Bold Women,

Big Ideas

Bold
Women,

PUBLICAFFAIRS
New York

Big
Ideas

Learning to Play

the High-Risk

Entrepreneurial Game

Kay Koplovitz

with Peter Israel

Published in the United States by PublicAffairs™,
a member of the Perseus Books Group.
All rights reserved.

Printed in the United States of America.

Library of Congress Cataloging-in-Publication Data
Koplovitz, Kay.
Bold women, big ideas: learning to play the high-risk entrepreneurial game /
Kay Koplovitz with Peter Israel.
p. cm.
Includes index.
ISBN 1-58648-107-X
1. Women executives. 2. New business enterprises. 3. Entrepreneurship.
I. Israel, Peter, 1933– II. Title.
HD6054.3 .K66 2002
658.1´14—dc21
2002017772

Book design by Jane Raese

FIRST EDITION
10 9 8 7 6 5 4 3 2 1

PHOTO CREDITS: *Launching Madison Square Garden Sports:* photo by Bill Mitchell Photography; *White House swearing-in ceremony:* courtesy of the author; *Amy Millman:* photo by Jim Walker; *Cate Muther:* photo by Steve Fisch; *Denise Brosseau and Kay Koplovitz:* photo by Steve Fisch; *Jim Robbins:* photo by Steve Fisch; *"The New CEOs": Krishna Subramanian, Lisa Henderson, and Kim Fisher:* copyright 2000 U.S. News & World Report, L.P. Reprinted with permission; *Jill Card:* courtesy of the author; *Susan DeFife:* courtesy of Susan DeFife; *Jane Homan:* courtesy of Jane Homan; Springboard Boot Camp: courtesy of Springboard; *Working the Deal:* photo by Steve Fisch; *Bruce Brandwen and Kay premiering on Broadway:* photo by Mark Boneau Brown; *Patty Abramson:* photo by Mary Noble Ours; *Springboard New England, 2001:* photo by Bobbie Bush of Bobbie Bush Photography

Contents

Introduction

It's a little like scaling a mountain that soars to 18,000 feet. Or white-water rafting a class-five river when you're far from being a world-class swimmer. Or scuba diving with the sharks off the Great Barrier Reef.

I know. I've done all three.

The difference is that unlike mountain climbing, which allows for some R&R between ascents, the kind of adventure I'm talking about, once you've launched it, never really ends. To succeed requires perseverance as well as nerve, savvy as well as innocence, plus the ability to focus single-mindedly, plus a kind of damn-I'm-going-to-do-this-no-matter-what-it-takes confidence. In sum, you have to be a little crazy. And you must have the thrill of competition in your veins.

Friends of mine say I'm describing motherhood. In a way I am. The great challenge of being a parent, everybody agrees, is that no matter how demanding children are on any given day, or how stressed and exhausted you become, the next morning it starts all over again. But this, I'm told, is more than compensated for by the miracle of birth, the joy of nurturing, and the delight you take in the steady growth and developing strengths of the child.

And so it is with a new business.

I'm talking about entrepreneurship, about the arduous process of creating, launching, and financing a brand-new enterprise. Although the principal focus of this book is entrepreneurship in the highest-risk, greatest-reward arena—the brave new worlds of the so-called information age—much of what I've learned and want to share with you, my reader, applies to all new and fledgling businesses, from opening a corner store to producing indie rock CDs. This goes for the case histories I have described in detail and for the practical dos-and-don'ts material in Chapters 8 and 9.

The United States, among countries of the earth, has been almost uniquely driven by the entrepreneurial spirit. Ever since those first intrepid explorers, backed by the venture capitalists of their era, set sail for our shores over a half millennium ago, we've been opening up new frontiers of wealth. From the farmers and fur traders of the eighteenth and nineteenth centuries to the first cyberspace pioneers at the end of the twentieth, we Americans have always had an entrepreneurial vanguard to invent new opportunities, new forms of economic activity, new means to prosperity.

Of course, this vanguard, historically, has been all male, and so are the high-risk investors—the venture capitalists—who have backed their enterprises. To this day, over 95 percent of American venture capitalists are men, and 95 percent of the money they invest goes to male-owned businesses. But a quiet revolution has begun to emerge on the American business scene, led by a new wave of entrepreneurs every bit as resourceful and determined as the old-boy networks that have heretofore locked them out. These newcomers are all women. I've met and encouraged and supported a number of them, as I will relate. I've watched their enterprises grow and, in some cases, die, and have come away enormously impressed. This book is about me, about them, and about the many lessons—some of them obvious, others hugely surprising—that coming generations of businesswomen can learn from our experiences.

The women entrepreneurs of today reflect the increasing numbers of women who came out of our business schools, our law schools, and our engineering schools and scientific laboratories in the last decades of the twentieth century, as well as those who found themselves stuck in midlevel careers in the great firms and corporations of the business world. They've been helped immeasurably by the proliferation of venture capitalists with pools of funds to invest in the new economy and by the relative ease of access, for women, to its fast-evolving high-tech and biotech sectors. But the challenges they've had to overcome have been enormous, and they too have been buffeted by the great economic turbulence and volatility of the dawning new century.

Getting from the proverbial "light bulb" concept to a fundable—and funded—enterprise is, as I shall explain, a complicated process in the best of times, and the learning curve is steep. But the one thing I'm sure of is that we as a group—women entrepreneurs—are here to stay. There's no turning back the clock. The obstacles we face may be real, but so are the opportunities, and, as I've discovered, we possess qualities that I think will help us flourish: for example, perseverance, passion, a gift for nurturing, and the willingness to network and help each other. These qualities will have as beneficial and, in some respects, as transforming an effect on the fast-changing business scene of the twenty-first century as the new technologies themselves.

Let's jump in, then!

1

If You're Not an Owner,

It's Not Your Business

Launching Madison Square Garden Sports

THIS IS A BOOK ABOUT WOMEN IN BUSINESS, PARTICULARLY about the new generations of women entrepreneurs. In recent years I have become a kind of beacon to any number of them in the fast-track, high-tech areas of the new economy, and I've come to care passionately about helping them pierce the veil of equity ownership.

In fact, I'm one of them myself. As I shall explain later, I am out there too, hell-bent on raising money for a great new business in the tough capital markets of the new century. But the truth is that those of us who are taking the high-risk road have wrestled with the same decisions facing all women who want to start their own businesses: Where's the start-up money coming from, excluding my credit cards? How am I going to cover the overhead—salaries, rent, taxes, utilities? How can I find good people to work for me—and pay them and keep them? How will I keep it all afloat until the revenue stream starts?

These are the basics we all have to consider, whether we're opening a shop, hanging out the shingle for a personal-service business, or shooting the moon with a technological break-through that is going to revolutionize (we hope) healthcare in America.

Capital.

Any start-up business requires capital, even if it's for the entre-preneur to feed herself and her family while she pitches her ser-vices over the phone. On a recent holiday in Puerto Rico, I ran into a woman who was staying at the same hotel I was and who, it turned out, wanted to start her own bridal-gown business. She had some business experience, and once she learned who I was, she wanted to know all about how to raise venture capital.

"The bridal business might be great for you," I said, "but venture capitalists are just not going to be interested in it."

"Why not?" she asked. "I think I can do very well at it."

"I'm sure you can, but equity investors, like venture capitalists, want high-growth companies that are quickly scalable and have the potential for a significant market share. They're looking to cash in with a sale or a public offering within a window of three to five years. Your business will require building a consumer market from the ground up, with Vera Wang and thousands of others for competition. It could take years."

"Then what am I going to do?" she asked. "I don't have the money myself."

"There are plenty of places to go," I assured her. "You just need to understand some things about the borrowing market."

I suggested that she might start at her local Small Business Administration office, where she could get assistance creating her business plan. In addition, there are nearly a hundred women's business centers located all around the country that are specifically targeted to helping women get their businesses off the ground. Not only would she find one-on-one counseling there, but she could also get leads on lenders interested in the retail, service, and food businesses. All of these are good markets, but they appeal more to debt lenders than equity investors.

"Debt lenders. You mean banks?" she asked.

"Banks and S&Ls, yes." And soon I was willingly giving her a short course in lending.

In fact, two banks with large national footprints, Wells Fargo and Fleet, have made a very strong play for women's business, and there are any number of so-called microlenders that have cropped up in the United States in recent years, probably inspired by the famous Grameen Bank of Bangladesh that has lent small amounts of money to millions of borrowers in the past twenty-five years. By far the most dynamic of these as a resource for women is Count-Me-In, a nonprofit, on-line, women-to-women "lending and learning" association founded by Nell Merlino, who also launched the "Take Your Daughters to Work" campaign, and her partner, Iris Burnett. Count-Me-In has raised millions of dollars from individual donors and corporations and is making micro-loans to women-owned businesses under a credit-scoring system radically different from that used by traditional lenders.

As I explained to my bridal-shop acquaintance, anyone with access to the Internet—and most businesswomen have it, as she did—has a great deal of exploring to do. All the women's business centers have websites, and all are ready and eager to dispense advice and give resources information and referrals. The important thing to remember is that times are changing for women in business. Although nothing is as tough as starting out on your own—whoever said business was supposed to be easy, by the way?—there's a ton of information just a click away and help at all levels, for all manner of borrowers.

But I made another point to the woman in Puerto Rico, and it's why I mention her here. Although the stories I recount and the lessons to be learned from them concern the high-risk, venture-capital end of entrepreneurship, *the principles are the same for all of us!* Unless we are independently wealthy (some entrepreneurs are) or have husbands with deep pockets (some of us do), wherever we go to raise money, we'll have to pitch our businesses. Any formal written loan application will contain elements of a business plan in it, so we'd better know how to describe our business and our goals concisely and accurately. We'll be interviewed too, and we're going to make an impression (good or bad). Our poise, our knowledge, our experience, our confidence—all these will be appraised.

But above all, as we will find out, many people are out there ready to lend us a hand. And there are more surfacing all the time.

※　　※　　※

FOR ME, AS FOR WOMEN IN GENERAL, IT'S BEEN AN ASTONishing evolution—or revolution. Think about it. A half century ago, Rosie the Riveter was sent back to the kitchen when the men returned from World War II and took up their old jobs and careers. The only professions where women predominated were nursing and elementary school teaching. Maybe through the war years our mothers and grandmothers got glimpses of different possibilities, a different future, but there were few women lawyers in 1950 and even fewer women doctors. (Harvard Law School, at midcentury, didn't even admit women.)

Still, when the breakthroughs came, they were in the professions and in small, personal-service businesses, while secretaries and gofers and "girl Fridays" (how I always loathed that term) began to climb their way into the managerial ranks of corporations. In certain industries—communications, entertainment, publishing—progress was quicker, but even there, with a sprinkling of highly publicized exceptions, the glass ceiling prevailed. Other industries—manufacturing, banking, transportation, Wall Street —remained totally in the control of the old boys.

When I joined the workforce in the early 1970s, women owned less than 5 percent of American businesses, generating less than 1 percent of total revenues. Yet by 1998, they owned 9.1 million enterprises in the country, contributing $3.6 trillion to the GNP each year and employing over 27.5 million people. Along the way, they demonstrated repeatedly not only that they were good at business but also that they were better credit risks than their male counterparts. And yet, as I found out when I started looking, of the billions invested by venture capitalists in new businesses the previous year, only 1.7 percent went to enterprises owned or led by women.

Only 1.7 percent!

The number shocked me. Behind it, as I would discover, lay a harsh reality: how difficult it was for women in business to attract and obtain financing from any investing or lending source. It was a reality, furthermore, that the feminist movement had by and large failed to address, and it was one I set out to change.

But there was a personal side to my motivation too. Although I didn't feel the bitter edge I've heard in many women's voices as they described their adventures and misadventures in the male-dominated worlds of business and finance, I learned the same lessons as they in my field, which was cable television.

Male-dominated? Hell, when I started out in cable in the early seventies, all full of ambition and competitiveness, it wasn't just male-dominated. It was *male.*

It also happened to be a field full of potential that few people recognized.

In those days, cable was what you subscribed to when you'd just moved to the country and your TV screen registered snow or jagged lines or double images or perhaps nothing at all. Unless you were willing to put up your own giant antenna at great expense, cable, for a modest monthly fee, was your only path to clear reception. In most parts of the country, it was local businessmen who saw the market opportunity; they erected the requisite antenna and set out to sell cable subscriptions to residents in their community. But a clear image was all you got from your cable company in the beginning. On the financing end—wiring a community, after all, required capital—investment was also strictly local. No venture capitalist—and there were some, thirty years ago—would have deigned to consider this cottage industry, even if it had appeared on his radar screen, which it hadn't. The business caught on nevertheless: If you wanted decent reception in a town like San Clemente, California, midway between Los Angeles and San Diego, you had no other practical choice. And soon enough there were mergers, buyouts, and a kind of gold-rush competition among cable operators who rushed to franchise every township, village, and municipality before their competitors could gain footholds.

Commercial television, meanwhile, remained firmly in the grip of the three broadcast networks. Local channels gave their viewers local news and sports, reruns of network shows, and Million-Dollar Movies. There were no superstations, no HBO or Showtime, no MTV or Nickelodeon or ESPN, much less a Food Channel, a Golf Channel, a Learning Channel, or a Discovery Channel. Only when the cable operators tried to invade the suburbs closer to metropolitan areas where there was clearer reception did they begin to realize, however slowly, that they had to offer prospective customers something new.

This was still largely the state of the industry in 1973 when my husband Billy and I took our road show into the woods of northern New Jersey and Westchester County, selling our cable system to the mayors and town councils of a slew of communities. We were working for a very smart entrepreneur, Bob Rosencrans, whose company, UA–Columbia Cablevision, was by then the ninth-largest cable operation in the country. We had twenty-six channels to offer in our basic package for a fee of $7.50 a month. For an additional $8.00, viewers could get something called Home Box Office, which had been started by a smart fellow named Chuck Dolan. HBO bought up rights for movies just after their theatrical run ended and long before they were offered to the networks. But HBO could broadcast them only in the immediate New York region, along with selected sporting events from Madison Square Garden.

All this was about to change—*explode* might be a better word—and I had the foresight to see it coming. In 1968, I'd received my master's degree at Michigan State University in an interdisciplinary program in international studies. My area of specialty was communications, and the subject of my thesis was the coming impact of satellite technology on communications, television, government, and society. The topic seemed pretty esoteric at the time. The first communications satellites had been sent aloft by the military in the 1950s, but they circled the globe at low orbits. Commercial applications followed in the 1960s, and the first geosynchronous orbiting satellites were launched, the same ones used today.

It wasn't until September 30, 1975, though, that the telecast took place that would truly launch the cable television industry: The "Thrilla from Manila," the famous classic heavyweight championship bout between Muhammad Ali and Joe Frazier, was transmitted 90,000 miles via satellite from the Philippines to ten-meter dish antennae in Vero Beach, Florida, and Jackson, Mississippi, and thence to television screens. The transmission passed its test with flying colors, to the satisfaction of the 200 congressional and industry leaders in attendance at Vero Beach. New programming—the forgotten element of cable TV—was about to come suddenly and dramatically into its own.

In 1976 the option HBO held on Madison Square Garden sporting events was coming due. If HBO didn't take it up, Joe Cohen of MSG was willing to talk to potential competitors. I had already left UA–Columbia to start my own consulting business, but Bob Rosencrans, my former boss, could be persuasive. He wanted to bid for the MSG broadcasting rights, but only if I would come back and run the show. "I'll do it only if you will," he told me. "You're the only person I know who can pull it off." At stake were 125 sporting events from the Garden, including the home games of the Knicks and Rangers, boxing, wrestling, and the Westminster Kennel Club Dog Show. All were now available for nationwide broadcast via satellite.

The clock ticked down on the HBO option. When it hit zero, the doors to the Garden opened wide, and in we walked. The result was the launch of the National Madison Square Garden Sports Network, which we announced in spring 1977.

We kicked off the campaign for the country's first basic cable network at the National Cable Television Show in Chicago that spring. By September, we had brought the network to 750,000 subscribers across the nation. For me, it was a dream come true.

%   %   %

BUT LET ME STOP HERE TO MAKE A CRUCIAL POINT. YEARS later, in view of what happened, I regularly got this question from people: Why didn't you hold out for a piece of the company?

It never even came up, I'd answer.

But why not? How could that be?

Good questions—years later.

It never came up in 1976 partly because I knew Bob didn't believe in giving ownership to executives. I figured we'd one day go public and that my equity would come. Otherwise? Well, it just never would have happened in those days. Not because I was a woman either, but because Bob was the boss and my mentor in the business, and because the equity was his, and because the launch capital—all $600,000 of it—was his company's too.

And me? I was the bright, determined upstart who'd just been handed the career opportunity of a lifetime.

The beauty of what we did, of course, was not only to bring top-flight sports events into the cable home but also in the process to create a new business model. Until then, television in America had depended entirely on advertising for its revenues, but we projected two revenue streams for the network—one from advertising, yes, but the other from our cable operators. Ten cents per month per subscriber. In another first, we got Bill Donnolly, national ad executive of the giant agency Young and Rubicam, to pledge $200,000 in advertising from his client base. Bill, a former Jesuit priest and something of a maverick, was willing to place a bet on the nascent sports network. This was exactly the kind of backing we needed.

My next step was to snag George Steinbrenner and the New York Yankees. The hated and revered Yankees! As a kid growing up in Milwaukee during the 1950s, I had been a rabid sports fan, and I was particularly passionate about the Milwaukee Braves. My mom and several of her eight sisters were sports fans too, and I maneuvered them into taking me to Braves games. That's when I fell in love with Henry Aaron. Oh, I loved Eddie Mathews,

Warren Spahn, Del Crandall, and a bunch of others too, but when Hank stepped up to the plate, I knew he was going to hit one out of the park—just for me.

So why aim for the Yankees? I may have grown up hating the Yankees, but I also knew there were people all across America who loved them, and either way I knew real baseball fans would watch them on cable.

The Yankees, of course, had their local television deal with WPIX, but when we offered them an audience outside the metropolitan area, it represented found money to Steinbrenner. We quickly negotiated the rights, and in spring 1979 the Yankees joined our network. We had a glorious opening game too: They played their archrivals, the Boston Red Sox, before devout fans from both camps, and the Yankees won on Roy White's home run in extra innings. Who could have asked for a more exciting debut?

But the euphoria of that inaugural game evaporated the next morning when I picked up the phone to a call from Bowie Kuhn, the commissioner of Major League Baseball.

Kuhn: Ms. Koplovitz, I understand your company broadcast last night's game between the New York Yankees and the Boston Red Sox, is that correct?

Koplovitz: We sure did, Commissioner. Did you watch it? It was fabulous!

Kuhn: I'm sorry, but you had no right to do that.

Koplovitz: I'm sorry, but we did. I have a signed contract with George Steinbrenner.

Kuhn: The rights don't belong to the New York Yankees, Ms. Koplovitz. They belong to Major League Baseball.

Koplovitz: But how can that be? George Steinbrenner—

Kuhn: Beyond a seventy-five-mile radius of New York City, Mr. Steinbrenner has nothing to say about it. That's where his territory ends and ours begins.

Koplovitz: But we're only talking about two million households, Commissioner Kuhn. Maximum three million. And if you insisted, we could black out any cities where there's a major-league game scheduled.

Kuhn: That's not the point. It changes nothing. Either you voluntarily stop televising the games, or failing that, Major League Baseball will be obliged to get a restraining order to stop you.

A *restraining* order? But how could I let that happen? I'd already sold the Yankee telecasts to cable systems all over the country! I managed to hide my shock and told Bowie Kuhn I'd call him back. Then I got on the phone to my lawyer-husband Billy and related the conversation to him. Is this possible, I asked? Can he stop us? Billy's advice was not what I wanted to hear. If Kuhn's statement about the seventy-five-mile radius was accurate, Billy said, Kuhn could very likely get a restraining order against us. In that case, although I might have recourse against the Yankees for having sold us the proverbial Brooklyn Bridge, my programming would have gone up in smoke.

Still, there is nothing like an inspiration born of sheer desperation.

I called the commissioner back.

Koplovitz: Mr. Kuhn, I want you to understand something. I believe I have a valid contract with the New York Yankees. I certainly liked what I saw last night. But if the league is going to persist with this restraining order, I have something to propose to you instead.

Kuhn: What's that?

Koplovitz: A trade.

Kuhn: I'm not understanding. What kind of trade?

Koplovitz: If you insist, I'll trade in the Yankee deal for a deal with Major League Baseball. I'll televise the games of all the teams.

Kuhn: All of Major League Baseball?

Koplovitz: That's right. Let me explain.

It took some doing, but out of that eleventh-hour conversation came a negotiation, and out of that negotiation—this occurred, remember, before ESPN existed—came *Thursday Night Major League Baseball.* Commissioner Kuhn, it turned out, was delighted to have his own found money, as long as it went into Major League Baseball's pockets and not George Steinbrenner's. Not long after that, we jumped into negotiations with David Stern, then general counsel of the National Basketball Association, for an NBA package, and with John Ziegler and Joel Nixon for rights to the National Hockey League. Within another year, we had over 500 live sporting events, most of them in professional sports.

By 1979 we had expanded programming to include a bloc of shows from Black Entertainment Television on Friday nights and from C-SPAN in the afternoon during the week. We quickly added children's shows and women's series, and in 1980 we changed the name to USA Network (and later to USA Networks) to better reflect our diverse program offering.

I was on my way, and I never looked back . . . until 1997.

I RAN USA NETWORKS FOR TWENTY-ONE YEARS. I WAS present, as they say, at the revolution—the revolution in programming and distribution that splintered the broadcasting monopoly of the networks and led to the diversity and multiplicity of choice that are television today. I was one of the leaders in a growing industry that benefited enormously from the new kinds of high-yield ("junk") bond financing invented almost single-handedly by Michael Milken at Drexel Burnham. It was Milken who backed people like Ted Turner, who built the superstation TBS into an empire that, after near-brushes with bankruptcy, he eventually sold to Time Warner, becoming thereby the largest single stockholder in the company; Charles (Chuck) Dolan of Cablevision, previously mentioned; and John Malone, who built TCI (Telecommunications, Inc.) into a cable powerhouse. I knew them all, worked with them all, and when our industry went to Washington to fight for our rights during congressional hearings, I was frequently among those who testified.

I was the working boss of USA Networks, and most of the time, I operated without interference. I'm naturally proud of all we accomplished; among other things, we successfully launched the Sci-Fi Channel in 1992. And although I certainly flourished as an executive in a mostly male world, there was that one important sense in which I was never permitted to play the game.

I'm back to the subject of equity. Ownership. To put it succinctly, the company that we launched with initial capitalization of $600,000 ended up being sold in 1997 for $4.5 billion.

That's right, 4.5 billion dollars.

If I'm not mistaken, that's a 7,000-time return on the original investment.

Logically, a piece of that $4.5 billion should have been mine. But it wasn't.

Mind you, I had tried.

In 1981, Bob Rosencrans's cable empire, with all its build-outs, came under financial pressure, and the threat of a takeover by Canadian interests hung over Bob's head. He had to raise cash in a hurry, and our USA Networks became expendable. I desperately wanted to take the company public, but Bob was dubious. Besides, he had to act quickly.

I was in Spain on vacation when he called me.

"I know you want to take us public, Kay," he said, "but I have this offer, and it's a good one. I have to take it."

The offer was $30 million, and it came from Time Inc., which by then, thanks to Jerry Levin, had huge investments in cable. Jerry wanted 100 percent of the stock. Initially, our working partners at Paramount (whose parent, Gulf & Western, owned Madison Square Garden) acquiesced in the sale, but Barry Diller, then chief executive at Paramount, convinced his boss, Martin Davis, to hang onto half of USA. Within the week, Barry brought in Sid Sheinberg and Lew Wasserman from Universal Studios (MCA), and Time agreed to a three-way split. The playing field shifted overnight, from New York to Hollywood, and I became what has been dubbed in the industry the "bicoastal exec."

I also felt a bit like Dorothy from Kansas. My still-small company suddenly had fifteen members on its board of directors, representing three of the great heavyweights in the entertainment and communications industries. Representing the East was Time Inc., then a formidable publishing house with cable systems and HBO as part of the Time stable. Time was a big player in the emerging cable industry and liked the idea of a programming network with a lot of original programming. The cast of characters included Jerry Levin, now retired as CEO of AOL Time Warner; Jim Heyworth, then CEO of Home Box Office;

Michael Fuchs, who would become CEO of Home Box Office; Thayer Bigelow, a Time Inc. executive; and Dick Monroe, then president of Time Inc.

From the West Coast came the two studios. Paramount was represented by Michael Eisner, now chairman and CEO of Disney; Barry Diller, now chairman of Vivendi-Universal Entertainment; Mel Harris, now co-president of Sony Studios; Rich Frank, the former president of Disney; and Art Barron, the ingenious general counsel of Paramount.

Representing MCA, parent of Universal Studios, were Sid Sheinberg, MCA's president; Tom Wertheimer, executive vice president; Al Rush, chairman of MCA Television; Bob Hadl, corporate counsel; and Charles Engel, a program executive.

And me.

Mind you, the trio of owners made strange bedfellows. They had just survived a protracted lawsuit against each other—Time on one side and Paramount, Universal, and three other studios on the other—over the pay-movie rights granted to the studio-owned Premiere Movie Network. Premiere had been launched by the studios, under the capable leadership of industry veteran Burt Harris, as an assault on Home Box Office. HBO, now owned by Time, was taking the country by storm with its offerings of recent movies, and the studios feared finding themselves at its mercy. After a series of skirmishes, the main battle was played out in court. Time Inc. won the suit, whereupon the parties decided it was time to make nice. That's precisely when USA Networks came along, and I often felt afterward that we just happened by the night peace broke out among the warring parties.

The peace turned out to be short-lived, and six years later, in 1987, Time Inc. decided it wanted out—at almost any price.

Here was my second opportunity.

I went to see Martin Davis, the CEO of Gulf & Western and therefore one of my three bosses. I was ready to pay $100 million for Time's third of the business—I actually had my backing in place—but I was also ready to raise $300 million to buy out both Gulf & Western and Universal as well.

And Mr. Davis, in his wisdom, turned me down.

Instead, Paramount and Universal joined forces. They agreed to pay Time Inc. $52 million for its third of USA. In other words, they got it for about half of the valuation I'd established.

Well, you win some, you lose some. In practical terms, all the deal meant was that I now had two bosses instead of three. And life went on.

Some years later, Lew Wasserman and Sid Sheinberg, chairman and president, respectively, of MCA, sold their company to the Japanese conglomerate Matsushita. Five desperately frustrating years later, having never understood Hollywood, the Japanese sold MCA to Seagram's, and Lew and Sid went off to count their money. Meanwhile, Gulf & Western trimmed down as a conglomerate and consolidated into Paramount Studios, which itself soon became the object of the affections of two media barons, Sumner Redstone and Barry Diller, who duked it out in a bidding war. Redstone eventually won and absorbed Paramount into Viacom, itself a growing media power.

The original agreement between MCA and Paramount, however, dating back to their acquisition of USA Networks, contained a clause that appeared to provide that any basic cable channels owned by or acquired by either parent company had to be placed under the USA Networks umbrella; in other words, they had to be owned equally by the partners. When Viacom acquired Paramount, therefore, it was obliged to sell a one-half interest in its two major television assets, MTV and Nickelodeon, to MCA and put them under USA management. But it never happened. Since Viacom had owned MTV and Nickelodeon prior to the Paramount acquisition, Sumner Redstone felt no obligation to share them. Besides, he'd never been known to sell anything once it was his. And when I once asked Sid Sheinberg of MCA if he intended to try to enforce the clause—after all, it did involve the company I ran—he replied, "Only if I have the stomach to spend five years in court fighting Sumner Redstone."

This was the situation under the Matsushita regime.

Once Matsushita sold MCA to Seagram's, however, everything changed. Edgar Bronfman Jr., heir apparent to the Seagram's fortune and mastermind of the MCA acquisition, was eager to prove himself every way he could as an entertainment heavyweight. Once he learned about the old clause in the agreement with Paramount, he demanded that Viacom sell him a one-half interest in MTV and Nickelodeon or, alternatively, sell him Viacom's half interest in USA. Redstone, predictably, refused. And Bronfman filed suit.

As part of the suit, Bronfman demanded 100 percent of USA Networks. And so did Sumner Redstone in his countersuit.

The legal proceedings hung over us at USA like a dark shroud. I did my best to keep the Sci-Fi Channel and our USA Networks franchise humming, but as time passed, heated charges began to fly back and forth, and as the suit wore on without resolution, I could feel the great company I had built about to be ripped asunder.

At the same time, I saw an opportunity—a way to break the deadlock and, in so doing, realize my old dream of equity. What if I could persuade one or the other of the litigants to sell out to a third party? What I really wanted, of course, was to buy USA Networks lock, stock, and barrel, but realistically I would settle for a share. The more I thought about it, the better the idea seemed. Quietly, in the spring of 1997, I began to do some prospecting in the capital markets, sounding out investors I thought might be interested. Before long, I'd come up with a plan, and I set out to test the waters.

I've often wondered what would have happened if I'd orchestrated it differently. Suppose I'd corralled Redstone and Bronfman in the same room. Suppose I'd gone in there, gunslinger-style, cash on the table, and said, "Boys, here's the deal. I'm buying you both out." Blowing smoke off the barrel of my Colt at the same time.

Well, I didn't. For one thing, there was no way I was going to get these two titans to sit at the same table, not with the court battle in full and public fury. Instead I took them on one at a time, one day after the other.

Day One was Edgar Bronfman Jr.

The Seagram's Building, on Park and 53rd, is one of New York's fabulous landmarks. Designed by Mies van der Rohe, it is an architectural treasure, an elegant gift to the city landscape from the Canadian company that, after all, was founded on bootlegged whiskey. Edgar Bronfman Jr., with his elegant clothes and good manners, clearly belonged there. He greeted me with his habitual politeness but also with a genuine cordiality, and heard me out in the same spirit.

We chatted about the lawsuit a while, and I told him how it was hampering my operations. Then I popped the question.

"What if you lose the case?" I asked him.

"I don't believe that's going to happen," he said smoothly.

"Well, look," I said. "Maybe you're right, but you might also be wrong. And I think I can extricate you from any risk. Suppose *I* were to go to Sumner and offer to buy out his half of USA. The way I've got it worked out, you could end up owning 80 percent of the company instead of 50 percent. I'd get the rest."

I worked through the numbers for him.

"It's an interesting idea," Bronfman said, "but Sumner will never sell."

"He's never been a seller, I know, but his position in this lawsuit is a tough one. I'd never underestimate his will to win, but he already owns great cable networks, even without USA. This could be an attractive exit from an embarrassing lawsuit."

"I doubt it'll work," he said.

We talked some more. I pitched and pitched.

But Bronfman shook his head. His answer was still no.

"No thanks, Kay. It's an interesting idea, I admit, and I appreciate your bringing it to me, but I don't think I have to do anything except sit tight. We're going to win the suit, I'm very confident of that. And when we do, we'll end up owning 100 percent of USA anyway."

Sumner Redstone, I expected, would be blunter. Viacom's offices, at 1550 Broadway, were as far removed in spirit from Seagram's as the Upper West Side is from the Upper East. Nothing sedate or slow tempo about the atmosphere at MTV and Nickelodeon, although Redstone's executive suite was large, well appointed, and decorous in tone.

I knew Redstone to be crusty and spirited and prone to jabbing his words at people, but he couldn't have been more laudatory and receptive toward me than he was that day. And he was full of ideas for making USA Networks a star in the Viacom firmament.

"I love USA," he enthused. "Great company, Kay. You've got a great company there."

Damn, I thought. While he was handing out gold stars, I was about to tell him I wanted to take USA away from him.

But that's what I'd come for, wasn't it? Undaunted, I pushed ahead, laying out my proposal to him.

His response, alas, was utterly predictable.

"But I don't have to do a damn thing, Kay," he said in his hard Boston accent. "Not a damn thing. We're going to win. We'll end up owning all of USA. Sure, if we wanted to start some new channel tomorrow morning, maybe they'd have a right to half. We might be willing to do that. But retroactively? To make us sell them half of stuff we owned before we bought Paramount? That makes no sense. It's not going to happen. Never."

Doggedly, I persevered, even switching the scenario to make him my eventual partner in Bronfman's place, but Sumner Redstone was having none of it. He wouldn't sell. And he didn't have to buy. It was all going to be his anyway.

Droit de seigneur.

In the end, I walked back to my office at Rockefeller Center in total frustration. Where to go from here? Nowhere. Without even a quiet maybe from Edgar or Sumner, who in the financial community would so much as talk to me? They'd rather sit on the sidelines and play eventually with whichever one of the two moguls won the legal shootout.

And I was out in the cold.

※　　　※　　　※

THE COURT DECIDED IN FAVOR OF MCA.

The very next day, Edgar Bronfman Jr. announced the sale of USA Networks for $4.5 billion. Under the deal, MCA (Seagram's) retained 45 percent of the company.

The buyer? Irony of ironies, it was none other than Barry Diller. Former head of Paramount, former head of Fox, and the bitter loser when Viacom and Sumner Redstone beat him out in the bidding for Paramount, Barry had been licking his wounds ever since and threatening to build his own entertainment empire, but he hadn't gotten much further than Home Shopping Network. Until now. Now, with the backing of John Malone, chairman of Liberty Media and TCI with its huge cable holdings, plus Bronfman with his 45 percent, Barry had just walked in the door and walked off with my prize.

Edgar and Barry held a 9 A.M. press conference to announce the deal. Then they headed over to my office. About 10 o'clock they bounded into my suite at 1230 Avenue of the Americas, looking for all the world like a pair of newlyweds and glowing with the thrill of their new partnership. Edgar, as always, was polite and somewhat formal, but clearly he was pleased at having brought his new friend Barry into the fold. He was brimming with confidence in Barry's ability to grow not only USA Networks but the studio television production and syndication units of MCA, which he'd sold him as well.

Barry, for his part, was beaming. He announced that he would be repositioning his odd collection of properties under the umbrella name USA Networks. Furthermore, he'd already decided he would be chairman.

"Now that you've taken the helm of my company," I asked him, half in jest, "and my title too, is there anything else I can do for you?"

This drew a nervous laugh from Barry, and the three of us joked about it for a few moments. But once we parted company, I knew I wasn't going to like his answer.

Several months later, Diller summoned me uptown to his office at Carnegie Towers. I knew this would be the day that my question would be answered. Still, even now, I'm stunned at the turn the discussion took.

We began by talking about different roles I might play at the new and improved USA Networks, though without much enthusiasm on either side. And then—this is the part I still can't get over, although in a way it was very Barry Diller—he treated me to a monologue of self-justification that must have lasted more than an hour. It was all about how hard his life had been the past couple of years, working out of a dreary industrial mall in Florida (Home Shopping's headquarters), and how he'd paid his dues—I think he actually used that expression—and how now, therefore, in summation, he had every right to want the trappings and perks of power.

Over sixty minutes of self-justification, and then came the punchline. I had the best job in the company, he said, and he wanted it for himself.

There it was. The other shoe had just dropped.

Even now, though, I'm not sure what he wanted from me that day. My approval, perhaps? Or my sympathy? Understanding? Forgiveness?

I'll never know. I do know that starting from scratch, I had built the first and certainly one of the most lucrative cable television franchises in the industry. And that, in the end, twenty-one years later, I was out on the street.

The issue wasn't careers now, or having had a good career, even a great one. The issue was ownership. And I wasn't in the game.

To the victor belong the spoils.

2

Ms. Smith Goes

to Washington

White House swearing-in ceremony with
my husband, Bill, and Vice President Al Gore

In my twenty-five years in the business, cable television had gone from the cottage industry of the 1960s and 1970s through the transforming years when Mike Milken brought his new kind of financing to a number of fast-growing enterprises to the maturing business of the 1990s when power consolidated in a relatively small group of large companies, financed by Wall Street and investment bankers. This isn't to say that newcomers couldn't continue to break in, but those who came to the table had to have deep pockets. I'm thinking of Geraldine Laybourne, who raised $450 million when she launched Oxygen with Carsey-Werner, the prolific television company, and Oprah Winfrey as partners. For the most part, by the time I left USA Networks, the creative, entrepreneurial spirit that had driven the business in its younger days had given way to corporate managers who represented owners like Rupert Murdoch's News Corporation, AOL Time Warner, and Viacom.

In the meantime, new technology-driven companies had begun to proliferate in brand-new industries that, in some respects, resembled the Wild-West, anything-goes atmosphere of my early cable days. These companies came out of nowhere and became—overnight, it seemed—powerhouses of the new economy in software, biotech, and most dramatic of all, the Internet. Along with them came a new method of high-risk financing that was to the 1990s what junk bonds had been to the 1980s.

Well, not entirely new. Venture capital, in fact, has probably always been with us. The great trading entrepreneurs of the sixteenth and seventeenth centuries—the East India Company, for example—were funded by the venture capitalists of the day, pools of investors who placed large sums, at high risk, in the hope of mammoth returns. Whenever, in human history, there has been a period of economic or scientific breakthrough—the golden age of exploration and discovery, the brilliant inventiveness of the industrial era, the communications revolution of today—investors have been lured by sudden and dramatic opportunities. The venture capitalist is often the first to recognize these new, volatile markets. He is at once a middleman and something of an entrepreneur himself. He brings together pools of investors and invests their funds in promising young companies, almost always in exchange for equity. Contemporary venture capitalists—I'll mention a number of them in these pages—tend to be young, male, and accustomed to networking in high-pressure, quick-acting, all-male milieus.

After I left USA, I became keenly interested in this confluence of the new economy, on the one hand, and the rise (or resurgence) of the venture-capitalist model on the other. I was interested in good part because I myself wanted to become part of a young enterprise where I could apply all I'd learned about running a business and where I would have that precious element of ownership that had been denied me in the past. But there was another element too—as much a part of this confluence of new social and economic forces—that took me in yet another direction.

That third element was women: women in business and specifically, the more I became involved, women entrepreneurs.

I'd always been aware of the problems women faced getting ahead in the business world, and in the past, I'd committed both time and attention to trying to help. I'd been a founding member of an organization called Women in Cable at a time when, unbelievably, only about ten of us were allowed by our companies to travel to national shows. We focused on providing women in the industry with better management experience and education and getting them out of the back rooms and into the front lines of direct operational responsibilities.

The Committee of 200 was another initiative I helped get off the ground, working among others with one of the great—and rare—woman venture capitalists, Pat Cloherty, to create a national network of entrepreneurs and executives who would act as a source and sounding board to up-and-coming women and provide access to large and influential businesses. Other organizations I participated in included Women in Film, Women in Communication, and American Women in Radio and Television.

At the same time, I would never have described myself as a dyed-in-the-wool feminist. Gloria Steinem I was not. No woman alive in the 1970s and 1980s could fail to be swayed by feminist currents or recognize the glass ceiling in corporate life, but I was more interested in trying to inspire women to reach for higher goals than I was in the feminist movement as such. I think I was too committed to my own career as well, too hell-bent on competing and succeeding in what I recognized as a rare world for women, but one I also loved.

Still, something had changed in me. Clearly the USA experience left its mark, not one of bitterness or anger so much as the growing recognition that for twenty-one years, I'd been lulled by being left to function as an independent, entrepreneurial type. As long as our bottom line grew—and it did, year in, year out—I'd operated with minimal interference from on high.

Well, we all have our illusions. The boys—that is, the Dillers and the Bronfmans and the Redstones and, before them, the Wassermans, Sheinbergs, and Davises—had always treated me cordially, had always lavished praise on my performance. As well they should have. I'd built them two great networks, had launched successful international businesses, and had generated cash flow in great amounts. But they had never, not even remotely, been ready to make room for me as a co-owner. Even though virtually everyone in the business equated USA Networks with Kay Koplovitz (and I did too), it was ultimately their bat, their ball, their game.

But once I'd faced this reality, unpleasant as it was, it was only a short step for me to understand that I had to change the equation, not only for myself but for other women. Even as I gravitated toward an entrepreneurial future of my own, I wanted to learn what women in general were up against and particularly whether the brave new businesses of the new economy might prove any different in this respect. Certainly there were encouraging signs. By the end of the 1990s, women would hold 46 percent of the managerial and executive positions in America, and although the glass ceiling remained very much in place, a few of us had managed to reach the top, with a marked skew in the so-called knowledge industries. There were Jill Barad at Mattel, Andrea Jung at Avon, and Marion Sandler at Golden West Financial, to name a few. But in one respect in particular, as I was about to find out, women had been completely left out of the loop.

At the same time, Washington came calling. The first feeler, in fact, came in 1997, well before I left USA Networks. It was from my colleague at USA, Iris Burnett. She was my head of communications and a Democratic party insider who had done advance work in several presidential elections. Might I be interested, Iris wanted to know, in chairing the president's National Women's Business Council? She thought I'd be perfect for it.

My first off-the-cuff reaction was no. I wasn't against pro-bono work—I'd always made time for it—but I'd been around long enough to understand that when the powers that be in Washington realize they can no longer ignore an issue but don't want to deal with it, they create a commission or a council or some similarly named advisory board. The statutory require-ments for this particular council only furthered my impression: a minimum of two meetings a year and the filing of an annual re-port. The annual budget was $200,000. From the sound of it, the council was nothing more or less than a political sop to women's interests.

But then, through Iris, I met Amy Millman, the executive di-rector of the National Women's Business Council, an incredibly hardworking and committed partisan of women in business. Amy was a font of information. She was also a political animal, having worked for years as a lobbyist on Capitol Hill for Philip Morris. She had politics in her blood, and now she'd devoted herself to working for women.

I didn't know that Amy had picked me up on her radar screen much earlier. I was one of the few women who'd made an impact on Capitol Hill and at the White House in my lobbying on behalf of the cable industry. In 1992 I'd been invited to Bill Clinton's economic summit in Little Rock, where I'd spoken out on the need to support women and minorities in their quest to build businesses and play a bigger role in the economic order. I'd ad-dressed a number of forums since then on pushing women ahead in business, one of them at the National Women's Business Council itself. In 1994 my friend Lillian Vernon, founder and owner of a highly successful catalog company, had chaired the council and invited me to speak to her committee. Before I testified that day in the hearing room of the old Executive Office Building in Washington, I listened to other women describe the problems they'd faced as they tried to establish the kinds of businesses that could be found on the corner of every Main Street in America, or on the kitchen tables of women working at home. Their stories were compelling, but was this, I wondered, what people needed to hear?

When my turn came, I scrapped most of my prepared words and instead found myself urging women—women in general as well as the women in my audience—to think big. I wanted them to imagine founding and growing billion-dollar businesses, not just million-dollar businesses. There was nothing wrong with a kitchen-table enterprise, nothing wrong with microlending and SBA loans either, but I wanted women to think about entering the private-capital markets to drive their businesses, to look for funding beyond their credit cards and their second-mortgage loan applications.

"Get into the game!" I exhorted them. "It's time for us to move on!"

The message seemed to galvanize the room. And one of the people who heard it was Amy Millman.

When Lillian's term was about to expire in 1997, Amy pushed Iris to sound me out for the job. They asked me to meet them for breakfast at the Hay-Adams in Washington. I was in town to lobby for access to capital on behalf of the American Business Council, a group of midsize, fast-growing companies founded by Arthur Levitt, who went from heading the American Stock Exchange to chairing the Securities and Exchange Commission. The issue of how capital for growth businesses was obtained—

and denied—fascinated me, the more so since I saw few women on the playing field. When I met with Iris and Amy that morning, I was energized by all I'd learned and eager to do something about it.

Apparently, I became their candidate that day, and they went to work in the back halls of the White House and Congress, making certain I would be the White House's first choice.

Finally I had a phone call from the president himself, offering me the chairmanship and urging me to accept, while Hillary Clinton weighed in via the grapevine of influential women we both knew. She, I was aware, had been greatly interested in microlending to women, the movement that had been highly publicized for its successes in impoverished Third World countries like Bangladesh. There was need for microlending in America too, for loans too small for commercial banks to bother themselves with. The Small Business Association had a special program devoted to it and, under congressional pressure, had started other programs to accelerate loans to women- and minority-owned businesses. The SBA was even underwriting portions of bank loans to these customers. Much of Amy's work at the council had been directed toward such initiatives. But worthy and important as these were, they weren't in areas in which I felt I could contribute. At the same time, as I told people up and down the line all the way to President Clinton himself, I would take the assignment only if I believed I could make a real difference.

I also talked to the previous two chairs of the council, Muriel Siebert, who among other achievements had been the first woman to hold a seat on the New York Stock Exchange, and Lillian Vernon. Mickie was a naysayer. I would put a lot of time and effort into the council, she warned, and end up highly frustrated. Even the members of the council, she pointed out, would be named by the SBA, not by me. The annual budget, she said, was so small that no one would pay attention to what I did.

By the time I talked to the president, I'd decided that if an emphasis on access to private capital, with no restrictions on my efforts, was acceptable as my target for the council, then I'd accept the appointment. And so it was agreed. President Clinton confirmed it. Then, because he was deeply ensconced in Middle East peace negotiations, he left the swearing-in process to Vice President Al Gore. This was perfect. If the heir-apparent Gore won in 2000, he would be all the influential support we at the council would need.

The ceremony was held at the White House on June 8 in the Roosevelt Room just opposite the Oval Office. I was pleased by the honor; most swearing-in ceremonies are not afforded the prestige of the Roosevelt Room. But this happened to be a strange day in the White House. The tension in the corridors was almost palpable—a function, perhaps, of the Middle East talks, but Lewinsky paranoia was also at its height. While waiting for everyone to arrive, including a number of friends and relatives, I walked out into the hallway and peeked into the Oval Office. The famous room seemed almost serene. It was empty at that moment, but it seemed to echo all those voices from the past, and I was deeply moved.

I wandered down the hall. There in the next room was Erskine Bowles, the chief of staff, a friend I'd met on a Young Presidents Organization trip to Russia in 1990. He was deep in conversation with Bruce Lindsey, a White House lawyer. Spotting me in the doorway, he nodded and waved me off. Apparently this was no time to socialize.

Then a staff member for Vice President Gore came to get us to brief us on the ceremony, and there was the vice president him-

self in the corridor. We engaged in some small talk before entering the main chamber, but Gore was visibly tense, and I noticed
that his knuckles were squeezed white. We knew each other from
years of lobbying when he, as the senator from Tennessee, and I
went toe-to-toe over legislation regarding the cable industry, but
on this day he treated me almost like a stranger. My husband
Billy, who often tries to loosen things up socially with some personal recollection or anecdote, pointed out to Gore that the two
of them had a long history of school rivalries dating back to the
1960s, when they'd attended rival prep schools in Washington,
D.C.—Landon and St. Albans—followed in Billy's case by
Princeton and in Gore's by Harvard.

They talked football, reliving some key game or other. Though
the subject held Gore's attention for a few moments, there was no
emotional response in the man. His mind was clearly elsewhere.

As though on cue, the aide rejoined us. She briefed us on the
order of speakers, and we proceeded to the podium for the
swearing in, which was a short but nonetheless stirring moment
for me.

Then Gore took the stage. He seemed suddenly lucid and, as
they say in the political arena, very much "on message." He
stressed the administration's support for the 5 percent target set
for the federal government's procurement of goods and services
from women-owned businesses. He cited advances at the SBA in
small loans and reiterated support for the SBA business centers
that offered women special technical assistance. It was all very
pro forma, but his delivery was sincere and convincing, and he
included all the latest statistics on women-owned businesses.

My remarks were brief. I wanted increased access for women
to private capital, and I had a plan to get it. I also told the vice
president we were holding him responsible for achieving that 5

percent federal procurement target. Since women-owned businesses were barely doing 2 percent at the time, I reminded him, we had a big challenge ahead of us.

I must unconsciously have delivered my comments with an implied wagging of the forefinger, because my challenge to the vice president was met with applause and laughter from the audience. On that upbeat note, the ceremony drew to a close, and Amy, our council members, and I went to work.

※   ※   ※

I TOOK A HARD LOOK AT THE CHALLENGES FACING WOMEN entrepreneurs in accessing capital, and what I found out floored me. The telltale statistics I reviewed are worth noting again: In 1997, women owned 9.1 million American business enterprises, contributed $3.6 trillion to the annual GNP, and employed 27.5 million workers.

Women were starting new businesses at twice the rate of men. Surely, I argued with myself, women must be making better strides raising money in the knowledge industries and the new technologies arena. In the more traditional service and manufacturing businesses, yes, bank debt was parceled out in dribbles to women borrowers, but in the new economy, wouldn't the old strictures and prejudices be diminished?

What I discovered was shocking, even to me. It was just the opposite. Only 1.7 percent of the billions in venture-capital investments that year, 1997, had been invested in women-owned businesses.

What did this meager level say about women? What did it say about our society? Did women somehow restrict themselves to low-risk, low-capital types of entrepreneurship—the family store, the beauty shop, the travel agency, the real-estate agency—and so pass beneath the radar of high-flying investors?

Or did venture capitalists refuse to invest in start-ups owned by women?

And if so, why?

The more I investigated, the more astonished I became. It wasn't just a case of one sex being slighted by the other. It was a universal and almost total disconnect. Nothing illustrated this more clearly than a breakfast meeting of the New York Venture Forum in 1998 when I heard Hans Severiens speak on the subject of entrepreneurship.

Since the mid-1980s, Severiens has been one of the most visible and written-about venture capitalists in Silicon Valley. Many of the storied VCs in and around Palo Alto had originally come out of high-tech companies like Fairchild Semiconductor and Hewlett-Packard. Severiens, a nuclear physicist by training, had worked for Perkins Elmer and the Atomic Energy Commission. In 1994 he and Jack Carsten of Intel founded the now legendary "Band of Angels," a loosely organized group of Silicon Valley engineers and scientists who wanted to invest in start-up high-tech companies. An "angel" had to work, or have worked, in high tech in order to join the group, but there were plenty of potential members because by the 1990s, significant numbers of engineers up and down the Peninsula, many of them still in their thirties, had struck it rich. They were sitting on cash—a person can buy only so many Ferraris—and nothing could have been more appealing to them than pooling their resources in order to invest in the start-ups of their friends.

The group concentrated on "angel" investing, a term borrowed from Broadway that commonly refers to investments in early-stage ventures that have already raised their first stake from friends and relatives but are still not ready for the $2 million-and-up level that attracts the venture-capitalist partnerships. The Band of Angels members—the number fluctuated between sixty and eighty—brought together expertise in a number of areas and were encouraged to serve both as scouts and judges of fledgling companies. They sponsored and promoted people they knew, people who came from the same background they did, and even, in some cases, people who'd come from the very companies the angels themselves worked for. In other words, it was the buddy system in high gear. Those who weren't sponsored by a member of the band need not apply.

At that breakfast, Severiens was justifiably, if rather smugly, satisfied with what his group had accomplished. In just the few years of their existence, he said, they had already invested a total of $42 million in seventy-four enterprises. Although it was too soon to calculate the results with total accuracy, he thought they were looking at an annual return of 30–40 percent. He was particularly proud that their $42 million in angel funding had been followed by over $200 million in next-round investments, some 80 percent of it from venture-capitalist groups, the rest from corporations.

The Band of Angels was a West Coast phenomenon. Severiens pointed out the hands-on nature of angel and venture-capital investing: At least one of their members, the group insisted, had to join the board of any company they funded. Thus they stayed local. Seattle was their northern limit, San Diego their southern. But he also named look-alike angel groups, modeled on his, that had begun sprouting in various high-tech centers around the country.

I was impressed, also a little dismayed. Hans Severiens has a way of making you feel that as long as you're doing things his way, you're in the loop; if not, why, you're completely out of it. Needless to say, I felt among the latter. But I had something else on my mind. At the end of the breakfast, I waited my turn in the cluster surrounding him. Then, catching his eye, I asked him if there were any women VCs in his circle of friends. No, not many, he replied, there weren't many. Then I asked what I really wanted to know.

"Of the seventy-four companies the Band of Angels has invested in, how many of them were owned by women?"

He looked at me a moment, speechless. Over his bushy eyebrows his forehead furrowed, unfurrowed, then furrowed again, as though to say, What kind of cockamamie question is that, and how am I supposed to answer it?

I repeated the question.

How many of the seventy-four companies were owned by women?

"I don't think any of them," he finally replied.

"Really?"

"No. None."

"Well," I said, "do you ever see any women? Do you ever get applications from women entrepreneurs?"

He shook his head.

"No," he said, matter-of-factly. "I don't think there are many around, doing what we do."

Next question.

Hans doesn't know it, but he launched a thousand ships in my mind that morning. His dismissive answer allowed me to see in a very real way what women entrepreneurs were up against and what we had to do. We had to identify women in high-technology sectors who were ready to build a start-up or who had already launched one. And then we had to figure out exactly how to make the connection between them and a world where they had no standing.

In my first months on the council, I talked to probably fifty venture capitalists and angel investors around the country, seeking to find out if they'd funded women and if not, why not. Most of them were men, but there were women too. And I always got the same answers. No, they hadn't invested in women-owned businesses. Few women, if any, had applied.

Of course, any number of "explanations" went with the observation. The most frequent was that women simply lacked the boldness and aggressiveness—the "balls"—required to raise money for fledgling businesses. But the following responses, in no particular order of importance, were also popular:

- Girls are less good at math and science than boys are. Whether this is or isn't true, the perception has been perpetuated in our schools, affecting the assumptions of teachers as well as students. As a result, the argument goes, few young women embark on technological or scientific careers, which is where most of the high-risk entrepreneurs come from.
- The motherhood factor limits women. If entrepreneurship, so it is said, is a 24/7 activity, 52 weeks a year, how can the woman entrepreneur bear and raise children? (I will come back to this one later.)
- Women have a natural conservatism. According to the psychological stereotype, women tend not to be risk takers. The statistics showing that a smaller percentage of businesses owned by women go bankrupt than those owned by men might suggest that women are somehow

"better" at business, but the numbers are also considered an "explanation" of why venture capital goes to men.

- Women, psychologically, are averse to giving up what they've created. Part and parcel of virtually every venture-capital deal is its "exit strategy"—that is, the IPO (initial public offering) or the buyout by another company—and, from the investor's point of view, the sooner the better. Again, the "motherhood" factor comes into play, this time metaphorically. Women, the observation goes, can't "let go" of their children. (I'll come back to this one too. It was a recurrent theme.)

- In contrast, many engineers, most of whom are male, are used to company jumping. Once they've completed one project, it's on to the next, wherever it is. Company loyalty is far less important than staying "ahead of the curve" in their field, which makes "exit strategy" for men who go the entrepreneurial route a very natural outcome.

- Women in business tend to operate through cooperation, negotiation, and networking. They are more passive, more deliberate. They lack that single-minded drive and aggressiveness that the high-risk entrepreneur needs in order to succeed.

Do you know something? Maybe much of this is true! Maybe most women do lack boldness and aggressiveness. Maybe by and large women aren't risk takers. Maybe they are nurturers and loyalists and can't let go. Maybe they aren't driven enough.

But can't many of the same things be said of most men? Since when are most men such bold and aggressive risk takers? Since when are most men so single-minded and driven?

The truth is that not everyone, male or female, is cut out for the entrepreneurial life, and that fewer still, male or female, are ready for the high-risk, high-reward, white-water version. The more I heard these "explanations," though, their increasingly familiar mixing of half-truths and self-justifications, the more I began to wonder if they weren't just a 1990s version of what people used to say about African Americans in corporate and academic circles alike.

"Blacks don't apply," it was said. "Believe us, we want minorities here in the worst way, but we can't find qualified ones. They just don't apply."

When you hear the same slogans and responses often enough, you start wondering if you're not barking up the wrong tree. What if there were no women entrepreneurs in the fast-track world? What if women—for one or more or all of the "explanations" offered—just weren't into high risk?

What if? What if? What if?

Well, as I was about to find out in the months ahead, there were plenty of women in America with the grit, the wholehearted dedication, and the passion to jump into the white water. Many of them already had. And some of them could well use a helping hand.

3

In the Heart

of Silicon Valley

Springboard 2000: Amy Millman, Cate Muther, Denise Brosseau
and me, Jim Robbins

FAST FORWARD TO JANUARY 27, 2000.

It is a Thursday morning, eight o'clock. I am standing on the high stage of the Oracle Corporation's conference center in Redwood Shores, California, in the heart of Silicon Valley. I am gazing out into the cavernous auditorium at a gathering that, before the day is out, will number in the hundreds, men and women about evenly divided. Some of them are venture capitalists, and I hope like hell they're ready to spend some money. Some—lawyers, accountants—have come in search of clients. Others are here to cover the event for print and broadcast media, while still others, people who have supported the effort in countless ways, want to see the "end product." An illustrious few are already stars of the new economy, women executives who will be honored and fêted at the reception that night.

Nearer to me is a cluster of trusted colleagues, most but not all of them women. They have toiled long hours and days and weeks on the committees to bring us to this moment of truth. They must be as nervous as I am, but not one of us is showing it. I'm feeling a little like a theater director when the house lights have dimmed and the curtain is about to go up. I'm excited, anxious, on edge. More than anything, I want to find a way to thank everybody who's made this event happen, and not just with easy words and the usual accolades that either precede or follow the main text of a speech. I will do that in my welcoming remarks; the words are already in my head. But how I wish there were a more personal and heartfelt way to embrace them with the admiration and camaraderie I feel for them.

But now is not the time.

Now is show time.

Behind me, in the wings, wait twenty-six women selected from over three hundred candidates—vestal virgins of the twenty-first-century economy. I know most of them by name, their personal names and the names of their companies. I have deliberately stayed out of the processes by which they were selected, the winnowing of the many to these select few. Similarly, I stayed away during the many sessions they had with their coaches, those drillmasters and drill mistresses who have made them rehearse and rerehearse their pitches. At least in theory, they now know how to walk and use their hands, how to manipulate the clicker that controls their slides, how to focus on the audience and hold its attention. Each of them will be on for seventeen minutes of presentation, but it has taken them many hours of dry runs to get to this point. One of them has already described the process as torture.

Are they ready? Are they *too* ready?

Who knows? In any case, it is too late to do anything about it, except cross my fingers.

Denise Brosseau is introducing me.

She finishes.

On with it, girl!

I'm familiar with this stage and with looking out over a sea of faces here. This is where Oracle holds its annual meeting, and I serve on Oracle's board of directors.

But now it's our turn.

I step forward toward center stage. Applause. Suddenly I feel welling inside me an enormous wave of optimism.

"Welcome to Springboard 2000."

░░ ░░ ░░

As I LOOKED BACK AT EVENTS FROM THAT STAGE, EVERY-thing seemed to have happened in a snap of the fingers. But a year earlier, in 1999, when Karen Bixby, Cate Muther, Jim Robbins, Amy Millman, and I got together on a series of marathon conference calls, all we knew was that we wanted to do something to bring women entrepreneurs into contact with private capital. How we didn't know. We'd been talking about holding a springtime conference to collect ideas and hash out the problems. Stick a hundred or more involved people in a single venue, with a fairly loose agenda and an open floor, and see what we could come up with by way of ideas. I had already decided the conference must be held in Silicon Valley, and as an Oracle board member, I'd already bent the ear of Larry Ellison, Oracle's CEO, about hosting it.

"Do you think that's such a great idea, Kay?" Larry had mused when I broached the subject. "I mean, women entrepreneurs and me? Aren't people going to take that for some kind of joke?"

He was referring—obviously—to his notorious reputation with women.

"Actually," I said, "I think it would do wonders for your reputation."

"Well, maybe you're right," he said, laughing. "Whatever you want, it's yours. It's about time we did something to put women in technology front and center."

Whereupon I booked the Oracle Center for April 13, the day after the spring Oracle board meeting.

The five of us I've mentioned formed a kind of informal Capital Cabinet, and we were joined almost immediately by a sixth, Denise Brosseau. All except Amy and me were from the West Coast, because we knew that whatever else we did, Silicon Valley—the mecca of venture capital—was where we had to start. We also knew we needed all the connections and clout out there that we could get. Karen Bixby was herself an investment banker, ran a fund with her partner, and was well connected up and down the Peninsula. Cate Muther, an alum of Cisco Systems, where she'd been a vice president, had founded the Women's Technology Cluster in San Francisco, the first high-tech incubator devoted exclusively to women entrepreneurs. Denise Brosseau had founded the Forum for Women Entrepreneurs in San Mateo in the mid-1990s, a pioneering venture in the same field that was to become a model for expansion to other parts of the country. Jim Robbins, whom neither Amy nor I had known before, was founder of the Software Resources Center, an incubator in San Jose. As it turned out, he seemed to connect to everyone in the start-up, high-tech field, and everyone—ourselves included—liked him enormously.

"Incubators," which were born on the West Coast and later spread across the country, were a side phenomenon of the growing software and dot-com industries. In exchange for a piece of the equity, incubators offered start-up companies physical space for their offices as well as certain pooled technical services, ranging from data processing to financial, legal, secretarial services, and the like. Some incubators also invested in the companies they sponsored and actively solicited outside investors. Jim, Cate, Denise, and others they recruited were instrumental in getting the venture capitalists of northern California interested in what we were doing.

As I've mentioned, the VCs of Silicon Valley had first come into being when the semiconductor industry began to explode in the late 1960s and 1970s. They had stayed out of the media limelight for a long time, in part because their activities were largely regional, in part because their firms were small—a dozen partners was a sizable company—and in part because their formal participation in any one venture was purposely short-lived. Their investment model called for placements of between $2 million and $15 million in any single venture, and their exit strategy called for an initial public offering (IPO) or a corporate buyout in from three to five years. Even though some of the great companies of the new economy had been venture-capital funded, it was only when Silicon Valley itself became the focus of intense media interest, and the semiconductor miracle gave way to the software miracle and the biotech and telecom miracles, that major venture-capital firms like Kleiner, Perkins, Caufield, and Byers of Palo Alto, led by John Doerr, entered the spotlight.

But what put these firms into high gear was the Internet. With the development of the World Wide Web in the mid-1990s, the so-called new economy grew suddenly and exponentially. Huge new companies emerged that nobody had ever heard of before, seemingly out of thin air. Many of them were founded by people recently out of college or, in some famous cases like Yahoo, still going to classes. Many were funded by VCs. The new dot-coms became Wall Street and media darlings; their CEOs, instant millionaires still in their twenties, were plastered on the covers of countless magazines; and "hits"—clicks onto websites—became far more important in assessing the strength of new businesses than were revenues or profits. As Michael Wolff described the hectic atmosphere in *Burn Rate,* his memoir of life as an Internet entrepreneur, CEOs of new companies, meeting at Internet fairs, typically compared "burn rates." A company's burn rate is the (negative) difference between revenues and expenses that can be covered only by fresh influxes of capital. High burn rates, Wolff wrote, were considered a sign of machismo. The higher the burn rate, the more successful the company's future was presumed to be. Otherwise, why would venture capitalists sit still for negative cash flow? (Why indeed.) By 1999, fueled by the skyrocketing stock market and the booming national economy, Venture Capital with a capital V and a capital C, led by the Silicon Valley firms, had become a whirling cyclone, sucking wealth from eager investors and flinging it, seemingly, at any enterprise that had had the wit to put a dot-com after its name.

Yet women entrepreneurs, as we knew, had remained out of the loop. This made me and the rest of the Capital Cabinet crazy, and the idea of yet another conference to air the issues drove us up the proverbial wall. Why did we need a *conference*? More talk, more discussion, more committees? Didn't we already know full well what we had to do?

We had to bring women entrepreneurs face-to-face with the investment community, and we had to make sure the latter took them seriously.

In one of our conference calls—I date it at January 14, 1999—the issue came to a head. Cate Muther suggested we forget about the conference and create the event itself—a real funding platform. Everyone jumped on the idea. By a kind of spontaneous combustion, we decided that the event should be a venture-capital fair or forum, one devoted exclusively to women entrepreneurs. Why couldn't we just *do* it?

I still have my notes of that call. They reflect a virtual torrent of questions and issues. What kind of fair? Where and when? How would we pay for it? How would we go about finding our fledgling entrepreneurs? How did we know there were enough of them, in the kinds of businesses that attracted VCs? How could we make them want to be a part of it, and how could we make absolutely certain they were good enough? Then too, were we talking only about Silicon Valley? What about the rest of the country?

No sooner was each issue raised than everyone started to talk at once, but in the tumult, several things became clear. Whatever we did was going to take the better part of a year to achieve. And we were going to have to get a hell of a lot of help, in addition to the kinds of sponsorships that would bring in the $300,000 to $400,000 of funding we thought we would need to carry off such a forum in style.

Whatever we did, we wanted to get rolling in a hurry. To this end, we started throwing names back and forth—who could do this, who was approachable for that? That particular conference call ran long, but by the time we were done, the decision had been made—we were going for it—and Springboard 2000 had been born.

Probably each of us came away with a particular worry. My own—and it was still with me that day a full year later when I stood proudly before our first Springboard audience at the Oracle Center—was where we were going to find the women entrepreneurs in the first place, and whether we could find enough good ones. What if the boys were right, the Hans Severiens and all the others? I thought that if we couldn't find twenty good candidates, we should fold our tents early. By "good," I meant women with real businesses, real business plans, real revenue potential, real management teams, and a realistic vision of what their companies could become—no, *would* become.

In fact, this was the very subject of one of our first debates. Jim

Robbins wanted to include angel-investment candidates, enterprises that had barely passed the friends-relatives-credit-card stage of start-up financing and were ready for their first, orangel, round of investment. This wasn't surprising on Jim's part. Fledgling entrepreneurs and angel investing were his business and his experience. Cate Muther's Women's Technology Cluster, based largely on Jim's model, did the same thing, taking a modest 2 percent of equity in the start-ups who joined.

But I resisted the idea, even when Jim proposed turning Springboard into a two-day affair, one for second-stage investors, one for angels. The earlier the stage of a new business, it goes without saying, the more problematic its future, and our biggest single obstacle, I argued, was to be taken seriously. At least for our first forum, we had to blow the minds of the old boys who controlled the purse strings. We needed winners, not maybes. We needed top-of-the-line entrepreneurs who'd already raised the first investment rounds and were now seeking venture funding in the rounds where real money gets placed. If we failed to make a powerful impression the first time out, I kept reminding everybody (myself included), there would be no second chance.

Jim, Cate, Karen, and Denise weren't daunted in the slightest. Cate believed she already had a couple of "maturing" candidates in her group. Jim and Denise knew of others. Yes, they agreed, we could come up with twenty "real" entrepreneurs.

Out of how many? I asked. How many applicants did they think we could attract?

Nobody knew. Denise thought maybe a hundred. If, that is, we pulled out all the stops.

Maybe I shouldn't have worried. Women had come a long way as top executives in the corporate world. I've already mentioned some, and in an amazing turn, in the course of that year, 1999,

Carly Fiorina would be named to run Hewlett-Packard. Hewlett-Packard was the quintessential Silicon Valley company. Once a start-up itself (in the 1930s), it was now the very model of the multinational high-tech powerhouse, and its antihierarchical management philosophy had set the style and tone of countless Silicon Valley workplaces. And there were the new-economy CEOs too, like Meg Whitman at eBay, Donna Dubinsky at Handspring, and Ellen Hancock at Exodus, soon to be the largest Web hosting company. For years a division head at IBM, Ellen had been fired by Lou Gerstner. Hired as COO of Apple, she had been fired by Steven Jobs. (Both of these events, it could well be argued, spoke to Ellen's credit.) Then she joined Exodus as CEO, nine days before its IPO, and she would drive this company with $12 million in annual revenues toward $2 billion at the close of 2000 and become a nine-digit millionaire on paper in the process.

(I'm well aware, as a footnote to the preceding examples, that when the bottom fell out of high-tech stocks in 2000 and 2001 and star company after star company failed to make its numbers, Hewlett-Packard was singled out by the media for special woman-bashing. Somehow, it was all Carly Fiorina's "fault," as was Hewlett-Packard's proposed merger with Compaq. To a lesser degree, the same thing happened to Exodus as its stock plummeted and Ellen Hancock left the company. And there were chortles in the same male-dominated business media when Jill Barad was deep-sixed at Mattel and when another company, Warnaco, led by Linda Wachner, filed for Chapter 11 and Wachner herself was ousted by her board.)

But all these women were hired guns. Where were the high-risk entrepreneurs? Suppose, for a multitude of reasons, white-water entrepreneuring just wasn't for girls?

In fact, women who were theoretically on our side, and who ended up working for Springboard, were among the naysayers. When I was out west that March, I met two of them—Ann Winblad and Heidi Roizen. They were major players in Silicon Valley venture capitalism, but their self-appointed mission that evening was to talk me out of Springboard. They didn't need an event like this, they said. In putting on a women-only forum, we would only be building our own ghetto. Any woman entrepreneur with a promising company would do much better going one-on-one with the venture capitalists. Ann was particularly direct on the issue. "We don't need any special assistance here. They just need to get in the venture loop and compete." Further, she argued, echoing my own worst fears, since she already had a pipeline to all the noteworthy start-ups in the Valley, we might find ourselves embarrassed by the quality of the companies that applied.

I was a little daunted by the strength of Ann's opinions. If someone wanted to talk television and cable and satellites, sure, I knew the ropes. But out here in Silicon Valley, I was a newcomer, a greenhorn on a mission. How misguided was I?

Heidi was much less emphatic. At least she was willing to consider the pros and cons of Springboard. She was extraordinarily well-connected, numbering among her friends many illustrious graduates of Stanford Business School, who form the elite of Silicon Valley. Steve Jobs was a former boss, and she counted Bill Gates among her personal friends. Heidi Roizen, now the managing partner of Softbank Ventures, was a person to reckon with.

I listened, and I debated. The arguments on both sides were in fact the same ones that had been used for years with regard to women making their way onto the playing fields of American business. In an ideal world, Ann and Heidi would have been absolutely right, and an initiative like the Springboard forum would have been superfluous. But we didn't live in an ideal world. The statistics proved that women entrepreneurs had been given short shrift in financing, and the experiences of people like Denise and Cate and Jim bore it out anecdotally.

In any case, it was already too late for us to back off. Soon enough, we were going to find out who was right, and it was a testament to these two good women that once we decided to go full speed ahead, they pitched in. Heidi Roizen, in fact, became co-chair of our marketing committee. A crisp and no-nonsense person, she helped us find people to set up our website and also the three-woman PR firm Eastwick Communications that set the stage early for a mammoth publicity effort. Ann never wholly bought into the idea, but at Heidi's urging, her firm, Hummer Winblad, one of the most respected in the Valley, became a sponsor.

I had decided early on that our first forum must be held in the heart of the venture-capital universe, but we also envisaged Springboards all across the country. There were high-tech centers in many areas—Texas, North Carolina's so-called Research Triangle, northern Virginia and Maryland, the Route 128 corridor around Boston, as well as New York and Chicago—and most had women's business organizations that performed a variety of mentoring and nurturing roles. We would need them as partners and co-sponsors, and so we began to seek them out.

We also had to determine what kind of forum we wanted. I had been to a few venture-capital fairs in New York, and Amy Millman had attended others around Washington. One of the best was MAVA, the Mid-Atlantic Venture Fair, a Washington-Baltimore event held at the University of Maryland's Dingman Center. *Red Herring* magazine held several fairs in the course of the year. At one point we considered asking one or more of them to join us as sponsors. But our impression, the more we looked, was that although the existing fairs did offer venues for entrepreneurial wanna-bes, with promotion and advertising (at a fee), the presenters were largely left to their own devices. In some cases, the focus was on panels and speakers, and the opportunities for new enterprises to present themselves and for investors to meet them seemed almost an afterthought. Anything the presenters got in the form of preparation and coaching was likely to be at their own expense and initiative.

We decided early that Springboard could never leave preparation to chance. There was simply too much at stake. The women who were chosen to present at Springboard were going to be prepped and coached and polished by lawyers, accountants, pitch coaches, and venture capitalists themselves.

Thanks to Denise, we came up with our name. We wanted something that suggested launching pad, jumping-off point, helping hand. For a while, with our high-tech target in mind, we toyed with On Ramp. But Denise's organization, the Forum for Women Entrepreneurs, had already registered "springboard.org," and the more we tested it on ourselves and others, the better it sounded. Denise, on our behalf, asked her board to cede it to us, and so they did. In that last year of the old millennium, a name with a new-millennial connotation carried with it a certain something, a resonance. So we became Springboard 2000.

All we needed were money and people. Oracle, in giving us the venue, would be contributing the equivalent of $150,000, but we needed sponsors who would kick in cash as well as kind. They should be local people, those with a stake in making Springboard Silicon Valley work. Again, as with so much of the organizing, a great deal of the burden fell on Denise Brosseau and her tiny staff, and again, Denise was up to it. The Silicon Valley Bank, led by Barbara Kamm, already sat on Denise's board. The bank would be our first local sponsor, with others to follow, and Barbara would take charge of our first coaching program.

※   ※   ※

ON APRIL 13 WE HELD OUR "STAKEHOLDERS'" MEETING AT the Oracle Center in Redwood City. We in the Capital Cabinet had been networking for weeks, trying to attract people who were well-known and connected in Silicon Valley. It didn't hurt that Laura D'Andrea Tyson was appointed to head the Berkeley Business School during this period. She had led the president's National Economic Council before that, and it was ultimately she who would get John Doerr, probably the most famous venture capitalist in America, to pay attention to us. We planned six committees with co-chairs for each (a safeguard in the event that one chair didn't pan out), and had one co-chair in place for each group before the April 13 meeting. To our surprise, whereas we had expected about thirty-five people to show up, over sixty did, and as we worked our way through our power-point presentation—What was Springboard all about? What was our timetable? What did we expect to accomplish? What committees did we need to fill?—I could feel the positive response coming from left and right. We had clearly struck a nerve, which was reflected not only in the good turnout but in the terrific enthusiasm and eagerness of those present to participate. Our committees filled quickly with volunteers that same day.

With Oracle, we selected January 27, 2000, as our forum date. There was no time to waste. We got our website up and running, and the screening committee set a first call of August 1, 1999, for applications from would-be presenters and a last call by September. Unfortunately, although the application forms could be downloaded from the website, we weren't set up to receive them on-line, so there was nothing to do but wait for the good old U.S. mail. A few trickled in during August. Meanwhile we continued to spread the word, through women's groups and professional groups and incubators and business schools and everyone we could think of, but for someone like me, who'd worked in the trenches of television, old fears came drifting back. Suppose the "ratings" were zero? Suppose literally not a single household tuned in?

The pressure was on. Nothing brought it home more than a midsummer cocktail reception that Heidi Roizen hosted for us on short notice at her home in Atherton, California, just north of Palo Alto. Twenty-five to thirty women were present, all of them from venture-capital firms—a good turnout when our research showed a total of only fifty-seven female VCs in Silicon Valley and San Francisco combined. We wanted to make certain these women knew about us, and we wanted their support, wanted them to become Springboard emissaries to their own and other firms.

It was a great meeting, one filled with a let's-go-do-it enthusiasm. But it also brought forth a message, loud and clear:

There's so much at stake. No matter what we have to do, we'd better not blow it.

Notice the all-important "We."

The omens, though, were good. Then we had a wonderful stroke of luck. Ever since I'd taken office at the National Women's Business Council and we'd decided to shift our focus from government funds to private capital, Amy Millman had been pitching the Kauffman Center for Entrepreneurial Leadership in

Kansas City to help us. The Kauffman Foundation had been launched and funded by Ewing Marion Kauffman, who had built his pharmaceutical firm, Marion Laboratories, from gross sales of $36,000 in 1950 to over $3 billion in 1989. A quintessential entrepreneur himself, Kauffman believed wholeheartedly in the entrepreneurial spirit, and the center he established in Kansas City had made important contributions to supporting and fostering entrepreneurial talent. In our view, what could be more worthy of the center's support than Springboard 2000?

But Amy had struck out, and so had I in my first efforts. The center just wasn't interested in supporting or funding a women-only initiative. Entrepreneurs, center officials maintained, were people, whether male or female was irrelevant to them, and the idea that women entrepreneurs might need a special kind of backing failed to impress them.

Nevertheless, there is no ally quite so powerful as one that comes from within.

In 1997 the Kauffman Center had sponsored am ambitious research project called the Global Entrepreneurship Monitor (GEM), jointly undertaken by Babson College in Massachusetts and the London Business School. GEM's mission was to "analyze entrepreneurial activity, its impact on national growth, and those factors that affect the level of entrepreneurial activity" in ten leading countries, including the United States. GEM's final report on its findings would not be published until 2000, but its observations and conclusions about America—some of them startling—became known at Kauffman during 1999. The Executive Summary of the preliminary report made these points:

> Culturally and demographically, the United States is quite distinctive. Americans accept and respect entrepreneurs; some busi-

ness terminations are expected and they are considered a normal part of the process. With Canada, the United States has the highest proportion of working adults ages 25–44, the age range of people most likely to start businesses. . . . *Further, U.S. women are very active in entrepreneurship, responsible for more than a third of all start-up efforts.* (My italics.)

This was the good news, and so was the report's conclusion that there seemed to be a striking correlation between healthy economic growth in a society and the degree of entrepreneurial activity. But the study went on to cite a problem:

The "Gap" in Seed Stage Financing. One of the more prominent problems identified by the key informants was the apparent gap in the availability of seed stage capital. However, key informants were in disagreement as to whether there really is a gap or not. Several explanations for this apparent contradiction were provided. First, if the gap exists, it may be more pronounced in certain industries (i.e., high tech versus low tech), different geographic regions (i.e., Silicon Valley versus the Midwest*), or for distinct groups of entrepreneurs (i.e., minorities and women).* (My italics.)

To this the report added: "Second, there may not be a gap in the availability of such capital, but, rather, *in the entrepreneur's knowledge of where it resides and how to tap it.*" (My italics again, and I'm sorely tempted to add a row of exclamation points.)

Could we at Springboard have said it better? The capital, we knew, did exist, and women entrepreneurs knew where it "resided." But they certainly didn't know how to tap it. This was precisely our reason for being!

More important, the Kauffman Center now took notice.

Whereas we had been preaching for months to deaf ears, suddenly people in Kansas City began listening. As quick as they'd been to say no before, they now became not only one of our most important sponsors but also our trackers and statistical monitors.

※　　※　　※

THEN, AT THE END OF AUGUST, THE TRICKLE OF APPLICA-tions became a river, and before we knew it, the screening committee was swamped. At the witching hour, more than 100 last-minute applications poured in, bringing the total to some 350. The numbers far exceeded our expectations. Clearly women-run start-ups in search of capital were out there—and in much greater numbers than we'd thought. Now the question was, Were they right for venture-capital financing?

In the initial screening process, about half the applicants were eliminated with relative ease by the graduate MBA students from the Stanford and Berkeley business schools who'd volunteered to help us. Those in the surviving group were invited to submit business plans. After a further sifting, the committee pared the number to slightly less than half of that group. These "semifinalists" were brought in for interviews, during which they made oral and, in some cases, electronic presentations of their enterprises before a panel of judges. The criteria for rejection were in many respects those a venture capitalist would apply: inadequate presentation skills, an unconvincing business model, deficient research of competition, limited market opportunities, or an unimpressive management team. The winnowing process, which was rigorous and required some hard choices, took the better part of two months, but when it was over, we had our twenty-six finalists.

Of these, twenty-three were technology or Internet companies; three were biotech. The dominance of the first group certainly reflected the spirit of the moment, because 1999 was the year venture capitalists' rush to invest in the Internet went over the top. Every day, it seemed, a new dot-com went public through an IPO at a mind-boggling multiple. Furthermore, this newest of the new-economy fields was, at least for that moment in time, the most open and democratic of arenas. People succeeded in it on their brains, ingenuity, and guts. Time and tide, therefore, were surely on the side of our Springboard twenty-six. At the same time, though, we had no intention of leaving things to chance.

At the heart of our plan were the volunteer coaches. Denise recruited many of them through her Forum for Women Entrepreneurs. They came from the professional ranks of the venture-capital world—lawyers, accountants, VCs themselves—and they became the true "directors" of our Springboard theater-in-the-making. Two were assigned to each of the twenty-six presenters. They met with their designated presenter two, three, in some cases four times, and reviewed her written and visual materials in between, including her business plan and her slide presentation. They also played devil's advocate, posing the kinds of tough questions the entrepreneurs could expect to hear from interested VCs. In addition to these volunteers, we had professional coaches in particular areas, such as Kim Marinucci of Winning Pitch in Palo Alto, to give special demonstrations and presentation workshops on everything from movements and gestures to how to avoid saying "ummm." It was Kim's suggestion that the presenters step free of the lectern, which was a place "to hide behind," and move freely about the stage with lapel microphones as they made their pitches. When the great day came, only one presenter remained behind the lectern—and that was because she was eight months pregnant!

Meanwhile, news of what we were doing out west had begun to spread. Amy Millman had been deep in discussion with people in and around Washington, D.C., and before the Silicon Valley event even happened, we were already committed to Springboard Mid-Atlantic. The Morino Institute, founded by Mario Morino, one of the D.C. area's great venture capitalists, was lined up as a key co-sponsor, as was Patty Abramson's and Rob Stein's Women's Growth Capital Fund, and we were already booked into AOL's conference center near Dulles, Virginia, for July 11 and 12, 2000. We were also looking beyond Mid-Atlantic, talking to Andrea Silbert of the Center for Women and Enterprise in Boston about a Springboard New England and setting our sights on Chicago and New York.

The money was finally coming in too. In addition to Oracle, we began relationships with series sponsors. By 2000 these would include Price Waterhouse Coopers, Grant Thornton, the Kauffman Center, Wilson Sonsini, Goodrich and Rosen, Silicon Valley Bank, and other corporate supporters far too numerous to list but who gave us the "people capital" as well as the financial backing we needed. We couldn't be sure how many venture capitalists would show up on January 27, but all of us were constantly on the phones, reminding and cajoling. Barring an earthquake, we were confident we would fill the house.

And we did.

But Springboard's fate lay ultimately in the hands of twenty-six women, from their late twenties to their forties, each of whom would have seventeen minutes to make her pitch. As I've said, I'd deliberately stayed clear of the selection and coaching processes.

I'd heard that we had a few relatively weak presenters and that Denise and her cohorts had been working them hard in the final days. Tempted as I was to peek during the on-stage rehearsals held January 26, I refrained.

But now it was time. Morning in Silicon Valley. Hopes were riding high. The audience had taken its seats. About a third were male. The heavy-hitting VC firms, I learned, had in most cases sent their women partners, if they had one, or more junior members, but at least they were represented, and if the big boys didn't want to come play with us, that was their hard luck.

Not even a minute left now for last-minute adjustments or changes.

I stepped forward to address the assembly. And then, within moments, it was up to twenty-six female, mostly first-time entrepreneurs, who were raring to go.

4

On with the Show

"The New CEOs": Krishna Subramanian,
Lisa Henderson, and Kim Fisher

First to take the stage was Krishna Subramanian. She was small and dark and poised and brilliant. She had earned her spurs at Sun Microsystems, co-owned five patents developed in its "New Product Initiatives" lab, and then had walked out, leaving her stock options behind, and founded Kovair in San Jose, a so-called B2B ASP, which in Internetspeak means a business-to-business application service provider.

As she put it in her summary, "With Kovair's VIPCenter™ solution, a company can create custom e-business websites in real-time for each of its strategic business-to-business relationships. The solution untangles the often-confusing lines of communication between a company and its customers, providing a dedicated, one-stop website tailored specifically to their needs."

With the help of a PowerPoint slide presentation, Krishna Subramanian confidently took the audience through the Kovair "solution." It included patent-pending technology—that proprietary, beat-back-the-competition feature VCs covet—and her company's only competition, she pointed out, was the in-house efforts of Kovair's potential customers to wrestle with the problems of communications on their own, efforts that were costing them millions of dollars and thousands of hours. Kovair, by contrast, could create custom websites within minutes with its system—as easy, she said, as sending an e-mail.

Krishna Subramanian walked the Oracle stage confidently, explaining, pitching, clicking her slides forward as she proceeded.

That morning, her company was all of nine months old. It had been launched the previous April on $1.5 million in venture-capital money and had fifteen employees. It was now looking for a round of funding in the $8 million to $10 million range.

And its CEO, Ms. Subramanian, was twenty-nine years old.

%%%   %%%   %%%

WE HAD PICKED KRISHNA CAREFULLY. IN FACT, WE HAD arranged the order of presentations to start and end the morning and afternoon sessions with our best candidates. We judged that Krishna had the poise, the understated savvy, and the presence not only to hold the audience but also to convince it that the overall enterprise—Springboard 2000—was something different, something it should pay attention to.

Seventeen minutes goes by in a flash, but it is also an eternity. (We would decide in future Springboards that, if not exactly an eternity, seventeen minutes was much too long.) But even before Krishna walked off the stage, we knew we'd picked a winner. Within a month, Kovair would raise its money—$9 million, the principal investor being NEA, New Enterprises Associates—and it is still doing a flourishing business as of this writing. But for our purposes, Springboard itself had now left the launchpad in fine style, and as presenter followed presenter, one woman after another striding confidently to center stage and pitching, pitching, pitching, all the hopes we'd shared were answered, and the work, the time, the effort, were rewarded.

The women came from up and down the coast, from San Diego in the south to Vancouver, Canada. Their employees ranged in number from 4 to 100. The oldest start-up was

Xenogen Corporation, a five-year-old biotech company from across the bay in Alameda that had developed an *in vivo* biophotonic imaging technology. Many others had been established less than a year. Some were in the more abstruse but no less intriguing areas of business-to-business "solutions," but many were casting a wider net in e-commerce, ready to sell services, products, and ideas to general-public customers over the World Wide Web. Best Self was one of these, setting out, quite boldly and unashamedly, to "revolutionize weight management"; e-style Inc. was another, selling fashion over the Net; and so was Eve.com, a purveyor of branded beauty products over the Internet that belonged to the famous Idealab! incubator, of which more anon. When Mona Lisa Wallace's turn came to present her ShopEco.com, out she came, wheeling a supermarket shopping cart filled to the gunwales with ecologically "friendly" products for the home that could now be ordered on-line from her website and drop-shipped by suppliers all over the country. The audience laughed in surprise at the shopping cart, but they listened.

And then, just before the lunch break, came one of our secret weapons.

Her name was Lisa Henderson, and her company, LevelEdge, was part of Cate Muther's Women's Technology Cluster in San Francisco. Lisa came onstage dribbling a basketball, charismatic with her spiked blonde hair, her infectious smile, and an electric presentation based on her own life story. She had grown up poor in Missouri, too poor to attend college if she hadn't wangled her way into a preseason college soccer game. The school ended up giving her a scholarship, not only in soccer but in basketball and softball as well. With three scholarships in hand, she was still obliged to sell her ancient car to get through college. After graduating, she went to work in marketing for Ralston Purina. Five years later she was in San Francisco, running Del Monte's Mexican operations. Five years after that she jumped into technology, heading the consumer products division of a software company called Audiodesk. Then, in 1998, she wrote up her business plan for a company that would use computer technology to match athletically gifted high school students with coaches in colleges and universities. It would, among other things, offer an alternative to the hustlers who preyed on the families of young athletes, promising them the moon in exchange for fees. As Lisa had put it in a pre-Springboard interview, "LevelEdge shares my vision of providing equal opportunities for athletes. I came up through the public parks system, not the country clubs, and it's much tougher if you're not part of a highly visible program."

LevelEdge listings were free to students, but coaches all over the country and their schools paid for their subscriptions. They'd started signing up almost from the day the service was launched. (One of LevelEdge's first clients was the famous Coach "K"— Mike Krzyzewski, the basketball genius from Duke University whose teams went to the NCAA's Final Four eight times in fifteen years, winning three championships.) A secondary revenue stream came from advertising from sporting goods companies. By the time of Springboard, Lisa had already raised almost $3 million, and she had Billie Jean King on her board as co-chairman. During her presentation at the Oracle Center, she announced that she was looking for $10 million more, and we had the excited feeling she was going to get it.

The day inevitably had its glitches. One presenter got stage fright when she lost her mental place in her pitch. The first sign of it was when she started clicking her way through her slides all the way to the end and back again. Then, in midstage, she simply froze, couldn't get another word out. I saw the panic in her face from the back of the room. Hoping to jar her loose from the grip of fear, I walked up the center aisle to the front of the room and asked loudly enough for most to hear, "Are your slides jammed?" She looked at me quizzically, without a moment's recognition. I asked again, "Is there something wrong with your slides. May I help you with them?" It was enough, just barely, to get her refocused, and she stumbled on through her presentation. I found out later that she'd been one of a group the coaches had been worried about—(there'd been another who cried her eyes out during rehearsals, saying she couldn't do it, but who, in the end, did just fine)—and it was likely she'd been overrehearsed. A major caveat in preparing presenters, whether for settings like Springboard or for face-to-face meetings with investors, is *never* let them memorize. The presenter obviously must know his or her materials inside out, but a memorized pitch, for nine people out of ten, loses all feeling and intensity. In addition, it can leave the presenter prone to the unhappy fate of this particular Springboard candidate who, it appeared, had lost her place in a memorized pitch.

A second glitch was overcome too—thanks to the Good Lord and Kim Fisher.

We had reserved the time slot immediately after lunch for our host, Larry Ellison, to speak to the forum, but lunch came and went, the auditorium filled up again, and the Great Man was nowhere to be found. He was delayed, we learned, at a meeting in the 500 Building where the executive offices are housed. We kept getting minute-by-minute reports that he was on his way, but thirty minutes went by and still no Larry. Then forty. The whole afternoon schedule was already in a major time squeeze. Finally, when he still hadn't appeared, we had no choice but to call on the afternoon's first presenter, Kim Fisher, CEO of Audiobasket.com.

Had it been anyone but Kim Fisher, who knows what might have happened. But Kim was an experienced entrepreneur—Audiobasket was her third company—and she had a stage presence that could have gotten her onto Broadway.

Out she came, toting a stack of magazines that she dropped on the stage. And then she went right to the subject on everybody's mind: Where was Larry? Probably, she speculated, he was in downtown San Jose. Why? Well, he was browbeating the town fathers into letting him land his Gulfstream at the local airport. He could use an "audiobasket" to get some dirt on the local pols. People began to giggle—Larry's feuding with the airport commissars in San Jose had already made the local headlines—and Kim had the audience with her as she segued deftly into her Audiobasket pitch.

Little did she know, though, that Larry himself had slipped into the auditorium. In fact, I was sitting next to him in the front row. And I faced an awful dilemma: Should I stop Kim and let Larry deliver his keynote speech? Or let her play out?

On the one hand, anyone who knows Larry knows (1) that he's not used to waiting and (2) that every move at the company is tied to his tight schedule. But as Kim regaled the audience, Larry joined in the laughter, and I decided to let her continue. Maybe, subconsciously, I wanted to punish him a little for being so late, but I also thought it would be great for us if he saw at least one presentation.

Audiobasket.com, which had already raised some $4 million in its first round of start-up funding, was somewhat like a customized *Reader's Digest* of the Internet. It allowed its subscribers to tailor the news content they received each day to meet their needs and interests. As Kim put it in her presentation, a user could choose to hear "(1) all the stories about the presidential candidates without any dirt on their sexual habits; (2) details on the Super Bowl; (3) business updates from Bloomberg; and (4) information on exotic travel destinations."

To illustrate, she pointed to the stacks of newspapers and magazines she had dropped on the stage floor. These were the media overload we suffer from that Audiobasket.com, with one click, was designed to eliminate. And then, as she paraded across the stage, pitching how the company could deliver its custom product, she suddenly began to unbutton the jacket of her suit.

People began to giggle again. Props were one thing, but stripping?

Then the giggles turned into gales of laughter.

The problem was, How to illustrate all the wireless digital audio devices on which Audiobasket could transmit the news—the cell phones, the Palm Pilots, the Personal Digital Assistants, and so on?

Kim swore later—at least for the media—that the idea didn't come to her until the last minute before she went on. But now, tossing her jacket triumphantly into the air, she showed the solution. All the twenty-first-century gadgets were clipped in a row to the belt of her skirt.

Her routine brought down the house.

Of all the presenters at the Oracle Center—and we had a number of talented ones—Kim Fisher epitomized the spirit of Springboard, one compounded of flair, resourcefulness, professionalism, and sound business sense, with a dash of comedy sprinkled in. It was no accident, when the publicity began to break, first in the West Coast media and then spreading nationwide, that Kim was one of the presenters in the forefront. And no accident, when we landed our single biggest media coup, the cover story on May 15, 2000, in *U.S. News & World Report,* that the trio of women on the front cover next to the headline "The New CEOs" were Krishna Subramanian, Lisa Henderson, and Kim Fisher.

"Meet the new generation of American CEOs!" read the subhead to the *U.S. News* story. "They're young, wired, fearless—and female."

〽 〽 〽

IN A SERIES OF POSTMORTEMS, WE REALIZED THERE WERE changes to be made before the Mid-Atlantic Springboard the following July. We recognized, for instance, that it had been a mistake to segregate the biotech companies from the dot-coms, obliging them to present their enterprises in a smaller adjoining room. We'd done it for the sake of the venture capitalists who specialized in life-science companies—and that aspect of it worked—but the biotech presenters felt isolated and in some measure shortchanged (though all of them were subsequently funded). We also recognized that a seventeen-minute presentation was longer than the venture capitalists needed, and possibly too long for most of the presenters too. With seventeen minutes times twenty-six presenters, the program tended to drag.

In the ensuing days, we would hear other criticisms from those who'd participated, which led us to change our format. Consequently, the Mid-Atlantic Springboard became a one-and-a-half-day affair, the first afternoon devoted to angel-stage companies, the second day to entrepreneurs in search of first-, second-, or third-round institutional investors. Also, the coaching and rehearsal process was preceded by a daylong "Boot Camp," in which the chosen entrepreneurs gathered to find out what would be expected of them. We upped the number of presenters to forty-four at Mid-Atlantic in July, then reduced it again to twenty-seven by the time we reached Harvard Business School in November. By that time, we'd settled on twelve minutes per presentation, and that is where we decided to stay.

The people for whom Springboard was only the beginning were our presenters themselves. Needless to say, no venture capitalists sat down, right there at their demo tables, to write out checks. All we could do, and had done, was to create a forum in which our entrepreneurs came into contact with the VCs. In the weeks and months ahead, it would be up to them to expand their seventeen-minute pitches into hour-long presentations, followed by one-on-one question-and-answer sessions that would make what they'd gone through with our coaches seem like summer camp. If they were lucky enough to have convinced the investment committee at the venture capitalist's firm, they would then undergo the "due diligence" process, during which every corner of their enterprise would be subject to scrutiny. Not only would the numbers underlying their business plan be crunched and re-crunched, but also their employees would be interviewed along with their suppliers and their customers, their bankers, their accountants, their lawyers. Along the way, they, flanked by their advisers, would be hammering out the deal itself, all the negotiable items and the nonnegotiable ones, down to the finest of the fine print, the entrepreneurs giving away as little of their companies as possible in exchange for cash, the venture capitalists seeking as big an equity bite as they could swallow.

I will come back to this process in detail in Chapters 8 and 9. For now, I want to reiterate that the road from the "great idea" to a solidly financed business with revenues and profits is fraught with obstacles, and the entrepreneur who seeks to build a company by raising capital is like a pole vaulter in a seemingly endless competition. No sooner is the bar successfully cleared than it is raised a little higher. Until you've actually done it yourself, no one quite recognizes how arduous and sometimes frustrating the process of raising money is.

This said, from a funding point of view, Springboard 2000 in Silicon Valley was a home run. By mid-2000 the twenty-six entrepreneurs had raised a total of $165 million. By year-end they were closing in on $200 million. Of the twenty-six, twenty-two were funded; two, who discovered each other at the Oracle Center, merged their businesses; one sold hers; and only one failed to raise money.

Stellar performance and great results, all in all, for a breed of entrepreneurs who'd never appeared on the radar screen. Right, Hans Severiens?

%% %% %%

THERE IS ALWAYS A DOWNSIDE IN BUSINESS, HOWEVER, particularly at the high-risk end. The fact is—as any experienced venture capitalist knows full well—most start-up businesses fail. Although they don't like to talk about it in advance, VCs build a failure rate into their financial planning. Their assumption is that one winner will compensate them and their investors for many losers.

This assumption was reflected clearly in the crazy, go-go euphoria of 1999 and early 2000. Many VCs I've talked to remember the period as a feeding frenzy during which the most dubious dot-coms with little or no revenues—but boasting of thousands, indeed millions, of "hits"—were propelled into IPOs at astronomical multiples, managed by ever-willing Wall Street under-writers, who fed in turn a public greed that bordered on hysteria. Some VCs are willing to blame themselves for their part in the craziness. Like everyone in the investment community, they knew the magic couldn't last forever, but meanwhile they racked up huge profits. Indeed, when the craziness is viewed from this side of the 2000–2001 dot-com debacle and the bursting of the Nasdaq bubble, it is amazing that the smoke and mirrors lasted so long. One could argue that some of the first Springboard entrants might never have obtained funding had they entered the financial markets a year later. But that Silicon Valley 2000 group, and those of the forums that followed, achieved an amazingly high survival rate, and at least some of the unlucky ones who fell by the wayside would surely have endured in a saner economic climate. In coming chapters, I give a detailed view of several Springboard alumnae who, armed with brains and conviction to go with their great ideas, managed to drive their companies through to success, even in the toughest of climates, with failure staring them in the face.

Nevertheless, there were cautionary tales that evolved out of that first Springboard, involving women entrepreneurs and their companies who got caught in the white water and capsized in the maelstrom. The most extraordinary of these—and it is a truly cautionary tale—is that of Eve.com and its co-founders, Varsha Rao and Miriam Naficy.

Varsha Rao had come to entrepreneurship from Harvard Business School, with a stopover at McKinsey and Company. Miriam Naficy got there from Stanford Business School, with seasoning at Goldman Sachs. Bred in the purple, as they say in horse racing, and when the co-founders hooked up with Bill Gross's Idealab! in summer 1998, their success in the go-go world of the Internet was all but foreordained.

Bill Gross was an early star of the Internet. A graduate of Cal Tech and Lotus Development, brilliant, fast thinking, faster talking, he founded a multimedia company called Knowledge Adventure and sold it in 1997 for $100 million. But Idealab!, a Pasadena-based incubator, was where his particular genius flowered—at least for the few years when his personal net worth soared to something over $1 billion. When eToys, one of his top start-ups, went public in May 1999, Idealab! held a stake in it worth $1.5 billion. The remaining $6 billion in opening-day value was owned by a variety of thrilled investors. Droves of VCs arrived in Pasadena by limo and helicopter, where they knelt before the guru and begged for crumbs from his latest brainstorms. The business media hailed him as the transforming figure of American business.

In addition to eToys, Idealab! start-ups from the period included Goto.com, CitySearch, CarsDirect, Tickets.com, NetZero, and Free PC.

And Eve.com.

Eve.com seemed a natural. Although the idea of selling high-end cosmetic products on the Internet, complete with advice from experts on a number of beauty subjects, was nothing new—among the competitors listed in Eve.com's Springboard presentation were Beauty.com, Reflect.com, Ingredients.com, Beautyscene.com, and Beautyjungle.com—the auspices were great. The brand name, Eve, was short and memorable. The Idealab! connection lent the start-up an aura of magic, and even before Springboard, the company had funding from Menlo Ventures; Charter Venture Capital; Weiss, Peck, and Greer; and Crosslink Capital. To top it off, its board of directors included Marleen McDaniel, CEO of Women.com, the largest "on-line community of women." At the time, Marleen was an Internet icon and one of our honorees at that first Springboard event.

Eve.com quickly became the leader in its Internet category—the Amazon.com of cosmetics, for better and worse—and in that magical span of time, from 1999 through the first months of 2000, the company seemed almost sure to be the first Springboard entrant to hit the proverbial home run.

Indeed it was.

Early in 2000, at the height of the dot-com boom, the company entered into buyout negotiations with LVMH, the French conglomerate formed out of the marriage of Louis Vuitton, Moët et Chandon, and Hennessy, which was then in the process of snapping up every purveyor of luxury goods it could get its hands on. In short order, LVMH made an offer.

The number was, as they say, "in the neighborhood" of $100 million.

Before Ms. Rao and Ms. Naficy and their delighted investors could catch their collective breath, however, Bill Gross entered, or reentered, the picture. Idealab! was not to be left out of the bidding. Gross made a counteroffer of $110 million for 80 percent of the company. Furthermore—his wildest mistake—he guaranteed $50 million to those inside the company who held stock options. In other words, after an eighteen-month waiting period, employees of Eve.com could cash in their chips at a minimum of their pro rata share of $50 million. To Varsha Rao and Miriam Naficy, this translated into a guarantee of $17.5 million. Each.

Done deal. Champagne for all. Goodbye, LVMH.

According to *Fortune* magazine, Bill Gross then—and only then—took a good look at the company he had just bought and discovered that there was no way he could make Eve.com work as it was then configured. Gross brought in retailing experts and, following their advice and with an additional injection of Idealab! funds, tried to turn the ship around. He also tried but failed to convince Varsha and Mariam to kick back their $17.5 million into the company. As for another infusion of outside capital? Where would he get it when e-commerce companies, the good, the bad, and the ugly, were being sucked inexorably toward the whirlpools of bankruptcy?

Finally, severely chastened and probably as much as $100 million lighter, and still presumably indebted to Varsha and Mariam for their guarantees, Bill Gross shut Eve down.

Meanwhile, Idealab!'s own public offering, already filed with the SEC and scheduled for spring 2000, was put off . . . and put off . . . and finally canceled. It appeared that Gross, instead of being content to play the game largely with other people's money (the venture capitalists' and subsequently the stock market's), had begun playing with his own. Idealab! had been built on the principle of investing no more than $250,000 in any one of its start-ups. Now Bill Gross became like a gambler in a casino, wagering huge sums in an effort to prove himself right. Eve.com may have been a big mistake, but it was far from the only one. And Wall Street, having determined that the bubble (largely of its own making) had finally burst, now turned away. At the beginning of 2002, it was reported that Idealab! was offering its creditors ten cents on the dollar.

And what about Eve.com?

Not long ago, out of curiosity, I typed in "Eve.com" on my searcher and clicked "Go." I assumed I'd get one of those ominous "disconnected" messages, but instead a full-fledged website sprang into view.

But it wasn't for Eve.com. It was for Sephora.com.
Guess who owns Sephora.com.
LVMH.
Touché!

5

Venture-Capital Dancing

Jill Card

SPRINGBOARD 2000 IN SILICON VALLEY WAS AT ONCE AN awakening and a coming-of-age. The notion of the women entrepreneur had heretofore carried a certain quaintness with it, symbolized by the mom-and-pop store, with mom stationed behind the cash register. The Lillian Vernons and Martha Stewarts of this world, starting their businesses in their kitchens, were a media staple, but in subtle ways their success stories diminished women's work too. If it was okay for a woman to triumph in business as long as she did it out of her kitchen, which was, after all, her historical domain (and God bless her for it), she still, so went the myth, couldn't cut it in the man's world of companies and corporations and boardrooms and business suits.

Springboard 2000, with its emphasis on a high degree of professionalism, exploded that myth.

But another wake-up call came for us in spring 2000. A reality check of a very different, more sobering kind.

The conservative experts of Wall Street had been predicting a slowdown for so long, and it hadn't happened for so long, that even the experts had begun to doubt their own expertise. Could it be, some of them had begun to ask themselves as the gold rush of the late 1990s galloped into the new millennium, that the business cycle itself was a thing of the past? Could the arrogant young apostles of the new economy be right after all? Had a new world— where speed, efficiency, and globalization generated wealth at an unprecedented and *sustainable* rate—suddenly come into being?

In the early 1990s, after the dramatic but brief stock-market nosedives of 1987 and 1991, the Nasdaq had risen largely in step with the "Big Board" indices—the Dow, the S&P 500. But starting in the mid-1990s and accelerating as the decade neared its end, the Nasdaq had literally soared out of sight. With it went the market for IPOs. Companies no one had ever heard of a decade earlier were suddenly worth more, in terms of the value of their outstanding stock, than giants like IBM, General Motors, and Shell Oil. Stocks launched at $20 a share were suddenly selling at $200 or $400 or more. Companies with zero revenues and red ink all over their balance sheets defied gravity like so many hot-air balloons. Computer geeks and Internet mavens with no business experience became millionaires overnight, billionaires in some cases. Luxury goods became mass-market, fancy clubs and elaborate gourmet restaurants proliferated, real-estate prices shot up, and these same instant tycoons invested in each other's enterprises, driving up their values. All it seemed to take in those go-go days was a "bio" in front of your corporate name or a dot-com behind it.

Wall Street gladly joined the fun. It should be remembered that the primary business of Wall Street is to generate wealth for its member companies and their managers and shareholders, and one important way it does this involves the underwriting and selling of securities and the organization of mergers and acquisitions between its corporate customers. Wall Street's task is to make a market and sell into it, and although Wall Street makes money when its customers dispose of their holdings, it makes much more when they buy and force prices up. If Wall Street didn't invent the Internet, it soon championed the dot-coms. It beat the drums and fanned the flames, and meanwhile it stirred martinis for the media. Profits? True, there weren't any, but profits no longer mattered. Revenues were good, and Amazon.com's founder, Jeff Bezos, won *Time* magazine's man-of-the-year award, even as his company gave new meaning to the old joke "We may lose money on every sale, but we make it up in volume." Revenues were less important than "hits." A "hit" was recorded every time an Internet surfer logged on to a website or clicked around the site from page to page. Hits, as a few astute observers pointed out, turned the stock-market play into a popularity contest, and popularity is what drove the highly visible but not necessarily viable companies of the new economy into the financial stratosphere.

Just as the gold rushes of the nineteenth century created ancillary wealth in the new boomtowns of the West, so did the dot-coms bring bonanzas for all sorts of camp followers. The care and feeding of the new entrepreneurs in cities like New York and San Francisco drove existing industries, like real estate, through the roof and created whole new sectors for others, like advertising and publishing, which rushed to market with a stampede of new magazines devoted to the new economy. Meanwhile, inside dot-comland, thousands of small service enterprises came into being, such as Web designers, programmers, graphic artists, and software engineers. Governments at every level—state, local, federal—rubbed their hands as tax money began to swell their coffers, and eminent politicians ran for office and often won on the sole promise of a huge tax cut. Unemployment was at its lowest level in decades, corporate productivity kept inflation in check, and with a national surge of millennial optimism came the growing sense that we could do virtually anything we wanted to do.

On March 10, 2000, the Nasdaq closed at 5,048.62. Cisco Systems, a tiny Silicon Valley start-up in the late 1980s but now the world's leading manufacturer of Internet hardware, attained a market capitalization of $560 billion, which at the time made it larger than General Motors, Citicorp, and Wal-Mart combined.

The euphoria had lasted for years, but now with brutal and dramatic suddenness it broke. The storm came in a torrent, the dam gave way, and the resulting flash flood swept everything with it. The CEO of Cisco Systems, John Chambers, would later liken it and the accompanying drop in business activity to a hundred-year flood.

In the immediate aftermath of the Nasdaq crash, with that Janus quality they have always exhibited in a crisis, the analysts and experts of Wall Street talked in terms of a "correction." Those who'd long since gone hoarse because they'd predicted the downturn for so many years felt vindicated. Those who hadn't predicted it said, Well, what do you expect? And when, in ensuing days, the Nasdaq dropped through 4,000 without stopping and, later, 3,000, the correction became a "severe correction." And what did you expect? One year after its high-water mark of 5,048, the Nasdaq closed at 2,069.89. This represented a loss of 59.3 percent.

Coinciding with the collapse were a series of disappointing financial reports from many of the bigger, stronger high-tech companies—Intel, Cisco, Dell, Yahoo, to name a few—and as 2000 gave way to 2001 and the economic brake left companies wallowing in unsold inventory, major cuts followed in the workforces of virtually every new-economy enterprise, large and small. Many dot-com companies went into total free fall and bankruptcy. Many ultimately closed their doors. The darlings of 1999 became the scapegoats of 2000, among them Priceline.com, Amazon.com, Yahoo, and Starmedia. Employees saw their vaunted stock options dissolve like vanishing rainbows. Then they lost their jobs. As 2000 gave way to 2001, not even a revenue stream was enough. Profit became the name of the game. Any company that wasn't on the high road to profitability was in deep trouble. And the terrible events of September 11, 2001, were just one more twist of the knife.

Amy Millman and I, however, and our many Springboard partners never doubted the overall viability of what we were doing. Individual venture capitalists might fall by the wayside; venture capital itself would survive. Even with all the cautionary tales told about investments washed away in the downturn, and of venture capitalists faced with the ugly choice of taking the write-off or sending good money after bad, there were billions of dollars in investment capital still available in the American economy. Further, to judge from the number of applicants to our Mid-Atlantic Springboard in July 2000, to the New England one in November 2000, and to the first New York one in March 2001, there was no dearth of fledgling women entrepreneurs ready and willing to take their chances.

This chapter and the next two tell the stories of three Springboard entrepreneurs. One presented in New England in 2000, the other two at New York and Chicago in 2001. Their enterprises— one in software, one in the Internet, one in biotech—are all at the cutting edge of the new economy. They illustrate a number of the ways in which the very nature of business is changing in the early years of the twenty-first century.

All three entrepreneurs have faced the pressures and the anxieties of being caught up in powerful economic currents beyond their control. Yet all of them have persevered. Beyond that, they and their companies are as different as night from day.

"IBEX PROCESS TECHNOLOGY," I BEGAN TO READ, "IS A DE-veloper of dynamic advanced process control software solutions for the semiconductor manufacturing industry using state-of-the-art artificial intelligence algorithms."

Dynamic advanced process control? State-of-the-art artificial intelligence algorithms?

What?

We had an unspoken rule of thumb in considering any Springboard application: If we couldn't understand it, the VCs wouldn't either. But here was IBEX, fifth on the list of companies to be presented at our November 2000 New England forum at Harvard Business School. I may have raised an eyebrow, but we have a second unspoken rule of thumb for applications: I stay out of the selection process.

So there we were, having just heard presentations from three Internet companies and one software, all of which sounded promising.

And now came IBEX.

She didn't look the part, this determined woman in black with a mass of black hair and a dramatic air, sizing up her audience even as they sized her up. I could imagine her on the stage of an opera house perhaps, but front and center at Harvard Business School? Surrounded by well-trained, well-kempt suits (male and female) with MBAs?

But then she smiled and introduced herself, and the minute she started to talk, all the anomalies disappeared, and the abstruse-sounding technology she set out to describe became crystal clear. By the time she was done, you knew in your bones that this particular IBEX was going to fly.

Her name was Jill P. Card.

What kind of woman goes the entrepreneurial route? It's almost impossible to generalize. At Springboard we've had our share of MBAs, and that's to be expected, for entrepreneurship has become a separate department in many B-schools and a highly popular one. B-school alumnae come with training in the business aspects of start-ups, such as how to write a business plan, how to crunch the numbers in a business model until they work (or refuse to work), how to go about pitching and raising money. They also enter the business world with at least the beginnings of connections and networks, thanks to their professors and their fellow alums.

But we've had more Springboard presenters who've never gone to business school, even a few who've never finished college, and I would be the last person to recommend to a young woman who wanted to start her own enterprise that she go to B-school first. I'm a firm believer in on-the-job training. Work experience, holding down a job, participating in an organization, learning to negotiate and deal with people in the complicated dynamics of a work situation—all these are more important, in my judgment, than the technical skills acquired through an MBA, many of which can be self-taught. In many ways, the MBA is a kind of insurance, but it's not essential.

We've had married and single women, women still in their twenties and others in their sixties. We've had many, obviously, who've wanted to make money, but we've had others—Martha Bridges comes to mind—who started their own businesses for other reasons. In Bridges's case, her closest friend—after doing everything right all her life, including medical checkups and mammograms at the recommended intervals—succumbed to breast cancer, and Bridges vowed, in memoriam, to help others avoid the same fate. Although she wasn't a doctor and had no experience in the medical-supplies field, she researched her subject meticulously and found the right inventors and an invention that needed commercialization. The product provides a kind of image-resonating test in which a woman, lying face down on a testing table, is monitored for breast cancer with much less pain and discomfort and, the company believes, far greater accuracy than afforded by the traditional mammography that failed her friend. Martha Bridges very proudly—and movingly—presented her new company, Interstitial, at the Midwest Springboard of May 2001.

A high degree of motivation is the one quality all our entrepreneurs share. These are deeply driven women. Some want to escape from corporate life, some to pursue a vision or do good in the world, some to make their fortune. But all of them are ready to make sacrifices of all kinds, such as working long hours at no or little pay. They share a quality of endurance, of perseverance. And they have guts.

All this I found in Jill Card, the founder and president of IBEX. But she had something more too, and it was visible even on the stage of that Harvard B-school auditorium. Jill Card is a nurturer.

%. %. %.

PASTED ON HER REFRIGERATOR IN WEST NEWBURY, MASSachusetts, Jill told us later, is a *New Yorker* cartoon depicting a Jewish family gathered for the lighting of the Hanukkah candles. The father is explaining the miracle of the Hanukkah lights, but instead of telling the story of the oil that magically lasted eight days, he says:

"The Internet start-up had only enough cash for one more day. But miraculously the money lasted for eight days, until more capital could be raised."

When she first saw the cartoon, Jill said, "I laughed till I almost cried. It hit so close to home it hurt."

I'm sure it did. Jill, like all the entrepreneurs in this book, has fought the money-raising wars that, for fledgling businesses, never seem to end. A mathematician and software engineer, Jill cut her teeth at Wang Laboratories and AT&T's Bell Labs, then worked thirteen years for Digital Equipment, the onetime computer giant in Hudson, Massachusetts, as a consulting engineer. She specialized in process control, in artificial intelligence recognition system development, and in neural network design and analysis—all difficult subjects for the layperson but that have practical applications in many high-tech businesses. While at Digital she was awarded a SEMATECH member share project sponsorship. SEMATECH is the university and industry consortium that was founded to promote semiconductor technology all over the world, a prime example of the key role academia now plays in many of the knowledge industries. Its sponsorship is both an honor and a seal of approval, and in Jill Card's case, it was one of the forces that set her on the entrepreneurial road.

In today's go-go business world, old ideals of loyalty between employer and employee have yielded to the pressures of the bottom line, and companies expand and downsize without qualm, notably in the newer high-tech industries. By the same token, once their particular project is over at Company X, task-oriented engineers try to stay ahead of the curve in developing technology by jumping to Company Y or Z. Some of these gunslingers, in fact, end up venturing forth on their own. But Jill Card might still be at Digital, having developed a useful technology there in the field of advanced process control and wanting to test, exercise, and perfect it, had not Intel taken over Digital's semiconductor facility at Hudson, Massachusetts, in 1998. Jill could see the handwriting on the wall. Digital, after all, was the second major corporation she had seen fold—Wang Labs was the first—and although she had never been laid off, big companies no longer offered job security. If there was ever going to be a time for her to go out on her own, she realized, that time had come.

In 1998 she founded NeuMath Inc., a small mathematical/statistical consulting company that served the biotech, biomedical, and pharmaceutical industries. In a practical sense, the change made little difference in her daily life—she had worked at home approximately half her time at Digital—and she soon had assignments from Ariad Pharmaceuticals in Cambridge, Abiomed Inc. in Danvers, and SmithKline Beecham Corp. in Philadelphia. NeuMath still exists, and it would serve as a useful fallback in the precarious times ahead.

But there remained the process control technology that Jill had worked on at Digital. It was hers now. By agreement with Digital and SEMATECH, she held "a worldwide, irrevocable, perpetual, royalty-free license" to the "optimizer" she had developed. In other words, the heart of her work was proprietary and protectable. Besides, Jill, and Jill alone, knew the code to it.

In this sense, she was a venture capitalist's dream.

The manufacture of semiconductors—those "chips" that have transformed our world—is a multilevel process, commonly involving over 400 individual steps from raw silicon wafer to the finished product. Each step requires precision of high order. Back in the dark ages of the industry, Texas Instruments used to advertise for workers who had keen eyesight and superb hand-eye coordination. Today, all such tasks are performed by machines, but machines too need to be tested for accuracy and consistency. In the fabrication centers of today (known in the industry as "fabs"), a test wafer is periodically inserted into the process and then subjected to detailed analysis to make sure all standards and specifications are being met. If they are not, all wafers processed since the last monitor wafer passed through must be either scrapped or reworked, and the process engineer then must decide how to deal with the situation based on diagnostic tools and his or her experience. Additional monitor wafers must be run and tested, and more after those, until quality control is finally achieved. Meanwhile, manufacturing has stopped, downtime accumulates, and the meter on costs keeps running.

Historically, the industry could absorb this expense and still enjoy its excellent profit margins. It had averaged over 15 percent annual growth in the three decades after 1970, and, including processing equipment manufacturers, chip manufacturers, and manufacturers of products that use semiconductors, it had become a trillion-dollar industry. But in today's globally competitive climate, there is a consistent downward pressure on pricing. Cost reductions and increased productivity are essential.

This is where IBEX comes in.

The IBEX solution, centered around its Dynamic Neural Controller, is based on Jill's work in neural networks. The following explanation comes directly from the company's business plan:

Neural networks are mathematical tools that invoke fuzzy logic and multivariate analysis to determine relationships between large numbers of complex, non-linear variables. They are patterned after the design of the brain's neuron network, which rapidly controls our response to multiple input.

A simple example: The brain recognizes the sex of an individual with a view only of the face. With a single glance, the brain captures information about the skin, hair, distance between facial features, etc. The neurons channel the information to the brain, which compares the inputs collected over a lifetime and determines the person's gender almost instantaneously. The individual is unaware of the vast amounts of data being input, processed and compared. Even when confused, the information that led to the confusion is stored in the brain, making determination of sex more accurate each time it "sees" another face.

Mathematical neuralnetworks work in a similar manner, rapidly capturing information, cross-linking and testing multiple variables and then re-linking and examining new relationships. The use of neural networks is made possible by the development of high-speed computers. Each time it receives a new variable set, the neural network scans its past calculations and outputs and learns. Even data that do not fit known relationships become part of the database from which future information is tested and compared.

Astonishing as this has always been to me—that computers could be "taught" to leave statistical methods behind, imitate the complex processes of the human brain, and learn from their own experience—I was also aware of progress that had been made in artificial intelligence. One highly publicized example was Deep Blue, the IBM chess player that had beaten Gary Kasparov, the world champion. But I was amazed to encounter, in a Springboard forum, such a sophisticated but at the same time practical application. IBEX's Dynamic Neural Controller (DNC) could "supervise" the functioning of a fab during a production run and rank in order the possible solutions to any preventive maintenance problem it encountered. Furthermore, it would continue to "improve" its diagnostic ability—just as the human brain does—with every run performed.

As Jill pointed out to her audience, there are some 600 fabs in operation worldwide, spread across seventeen major companies, with new ones being added at the rate of about twenty-five a year. A Texas Instruments study of 1997 had indicated that as much as $135 million *per year per fab* could be saved by the use of advanced process and equipment control solutions. This was real money, and IBEX, in its business plan, was forecasting a future with big revenues and major profits. But where there is real money and revenues and profits, didn't there have to be competition?

Of course there was. Advanced process control had already become a catchphrase in semiconductor circles, but the big companies had tended to outsource the research. Even as Jill identified four existing or potential competitors—a sine qua non in presenting an enterprise to venture capitalists—she was convinced IBEX would compete effectively. Her system was more "robust"—a favorite word of hers—and offered more value to the fabs. Furthermore, major companies in the field were lining up to evaluate it.

IBM, Lucent, ST Microelectronics, Applied Materials, and a half dozen others wanted to test Jill's product, and even before her Springboard presentation, beta testing had been organized for early 2001. One test, under SEMATECH auspices, would take place at the Lucent Technologies site in Orlando, Florida, another with ST Microelectronics in Phoenix, Arizona. A third had been agreed to with IBM at its Essex Junction, Vermont, facility. IBM, being IBM, made clear that it was neither endorsing nor recommending the DNC, but it had agreed to give other potential customers access to view it and fact-find, and it was probable, if the DNC "passed," that IBM would consider it for purchase.

This was the state of the company when Jill Card stepped forward onto the Harvard Business School stage in November 2000. She had every reason to be confident, and her confidence made her description of high technology sing, almost like a poet giving access to a strange and unknown and inexplicable world.

⁓⁓   ⁓⁓   ⁓⁓

BUT THERE WAS MORE TO JILL CARD'S STORY THAN THAT of a very talented entrepreneur trafficking in a male sphere and willing to take the same risks. Call it the human side, the cartoon-on-the-refrigerator side. She had a family, for one thing—a husband, two teenage children, plus two dogs and six cats. In addition, two other teenage girls, for separate and unofficial reasons, lived with the family in the early days of IBEX.

How did Jill do it all, the family, the house, the children, the husband, and the constant 24/7 demands of an exciting new enterprise? Did she have to be Superwoman?

The answer was no.

Here is the way Jill put it (not on stage at the Harvard Business School but in subsequent conversations and correspondence):

My mantra for the many crises that crop up in the business is simply "It is never the end of the world, no matter how much it would appear at this moment to be so." I firmly realize that if I'm not balanced and emotionally at rest, then everything suffers, including the business. So the time to go to the gym with my husband and son is found, the time to go to Utah [where Jill's daughter now lives] is found. On the other hand, when I am working, I am working, whether it's at the office or at home. I always worked at least fifty percent from home during my Digital Equipment years. Husband and kids knew that if my home office door was shut, they knocked at their own risk. I was—and am—on the phone constantly and might well wave them off. When their crises surpassed all, they wrote me a note and shoved it under my nose. Otherwise, they saved it and talked to me when I came out at day's end.

The idea of balance—of finding a way to handle the many demands of both business and family life—is one I've run into constantly in talking to women entrepreneurs. Women about to take the entrepreneurial plunge often bring it up, and if they don't, I sometimes do. There are those who have begun to hear the biological clock ticking and balk at the tremendous demands of starting their own businesses. There are others who try to put the clock under a pillow. Deanna Brown, a personable and attractive businesswoman in her thirties, who was CEO of Inside.com before it was sold to Steven Brill's magazine-cum-Internet group, said she had just begun to hear the clock ticking but didn't know how to find the balance between marriage and motherhood, on the one hand, and the demands of a start-up business on the other. "For the past three years," Deanna said, "I've been working seven days a week, ten to twelve hours a day. And loving it."

Fred Wilson, the New York capitalist whose firm, Flatiron Partners, had been a major investor in Deanna Brown's company, believes the reason there aren't more women entrepreneurs looking for venture capital is that women in their late twenties to early forties, the prime period for entrepreneurship, are also precisely in their prime childbearing years. Comments like that make the hair of women in business stand straight up—sorry, Fred—but he's correct in that doing both requires a juggling act that daunts some women before they even try.

Nevertheless, many women do summon the resources to succeed on both fronts. Rebecca MacKinnon, president, CEO, and founder of BeyondNow Technologies, had two infant children when in 1994 she spun her business out of Kansas City Hospice, for which she had worked. BeyondNow is a backroom service in the healthcare field, and Rebecca has won recognition from Ernst and Young's Entrepreneur of the Year, Deloitte & Touche's Fast 50, and the Smithsonian Institute for Information Technologies. She has also built her business to the profitability stage, when venture capital becomes an option, not a necessity.

When we asked Rebecca how she'd managed the juggling act, she replied: "The balance of motherhood and entrepreneurship is tough. I struggled with the insatiable desire to build this business and the competing demands of my family. I could never have done both had it not been for my husband at the time, who was a very dedicated father." Although she and her husband have since divorced, they continue to share and cooperate in bringing up their kids, and Rebecca continues to carve out the hours to run and build her company. When we asked her, as we do all Springboard alumnae, what counsel she would give to other women who were considering entrepreneurship, she answered with her characteristic honesty and forthrightness: "Know what you are walking into. It is work, and it is a risk to your family life. However, it is very much worth it."

The Springboard experience has taught us that there are any number of women ready to walk in and with their eyes open. Some of them are already mothers. Some are almost-mothers. I believe we've averaged at least one pregnant presenter at each of our Springboard forums.

As for me, I can claim no expertise on how to achieve the balance these women talk about. For one thing, my husband and I have no children. For another, I have run into countless variations on how women strive for that balance and, at least in some cases, achieve it. All I know is that every time one of our pregnant entrepreneurs walks to center stage and begins pitching her company, I feel a great welling of pride.

WHEN WE ASKED JILL CARD WHY SHE HAD STARTED ON HER own and, with a smile, suggested greed—a plausible and acceptable motive for any entrepreneur—Jill said greed had not been a factor. It was all about autonomy and personal satisfaction. "I love data!" she said. "Sinking into a data set for me is like taking a luxurious bubble bath."

And then she elaborated:

I also wanted to found a small organization that treated all its employees the way I'd wanted to be treated. This is very important to me. IBEX's new employees all receive little laughing Buddhas to put on their desks (if they want to). He is Poe-Tai Hoshang, a Chinese Zen master who lived in the sixth century, and he is worshiped for happiness and good fortune. My particular Buddha has a little bell inside. The idea is that when you pick it up and hear it, it centers you and makes you think about making the best of the day or the situation confronting you. Maybe that's corny, but I want people to realize that it never is the end of the world, that all difficulties can somehow be handled with grace and respect. I am learning how to do that every day, always with the help of those I work with or am doing business with.

Wow.

Was this woman for real? How could she make it in the cut-throat world of business? Wouldn't she get eaten alive?

And who among those cruelest of cruel, the venture capitalists, would ever invest in IBEX, even if it had found the secret (patentable and scalable) to eternal life and wealth?

Jill's first investor, after she'd started NeuMath but before she launched IBEX, was her mentor, Dr. Param Singh. He pledged the first $100,000 for IBEX, but with the proviso that Jill raise a matching amount before he signed the check. Smart man. Much as he was sold on Jill's concept and its commercial potential, he needed to make sure she could pitch her company successfully to others. Through Singh, she met and convinced a small local group of private investors, who kicked in another $70,000. Then FabCentric Inc., itself a start-up company that was providing interface services within the semiconductor APC world, saw mutual interest and potential value in collaborating with IBEX and invested $150,000 during IBEX's first six months of life. Another $60,000 came from private individuals who'd been working as consultants to the project. Most of these sums dribbled in over the first nine months after the company's creation, often just in time to meet payroll. In addition, Jill and her husband, Jerry, took out an equity loan on their home. It was a time when miracles had to happen—like the stretching of the Hanukkah oil.

Jill began making presentations to venture capitalists in June 2000. Before she closed her first round in early January 2001, she presented to fifteen different groups, drawing from the first presentations clues to what critical pieces she had to have in place—the clear marketing strategy, the detailed financials, the filled-out management team, the relationships with future customers, and so on. There were catch-22 aspects to the exercise, highly frustrating dilemmas such as how to achieve everything she needed in order to attract funding without having the funding to achieve it. But there was also a learning curve. The Springboard experience added to it. "I got direct, fantastic coaching," Jill said later, "and I met a whole bevy of businesswomen throughout the Boston area. As one who'd worked in a male-dominated field, that wowed me. Springboard also got me connected with legal orgs, marketing orgs, banks, investment bankers, VCs, et cetera, all forms of services that we needed to grow the business that I didn't even know existed."

During a coaching session at the beginning of November 2000, about ten days before the Springboard forum, Ollie Curme, a venture capitalist with Battery Ventures, heard Jill's pitch and jumped. How, he wanted to know, could Battery get on board in a big way before the forum was held? Curme and his colleagues did an amazingly fast initial due diligence, and he and Jill signed a term sheet between them, bringing in another venture firm called Warbros just minutes before Jill walked on stage at the Harvard Business School. I didn't know this at the time, nor did I know that she was carrying the signing pen with her as a prop, but it's no wonder there was a glow about her pitch.

Still, it was a near thing.

Before Battery Ventures would sign the final deal, its negotiators insisted that Jill find funding on the West Coast too, in the heart of the semiconductor industry. This was smart business. If Silicon Valley saw no future in IBEX, how could a New England VC firm? Battery also helped Jill find potential partners who specialized in her area of technology. But during December she found herself on red-eye flights back and forth so often, coast to coast, pitching as she went, that she virtually lost track of day and night. And she almost didn't make it. Again, in Jill's words:

> There was one point that December when I thought we were sunk and I wasn't going to be able to pay the people I owed back salary to. That was the only time I cried. But I never really thought of quitting. I did think we might have to close up shop temporarily and get consulting contracts to support us through. I was afraid we'd lose a lot of steam, though, given the likelihood that our initial team of four would have had to break up to find food money. But I never quite ran out of ideas on how to tackle the latest emergency requirement. Whom to call, another angle to pursue, et cetera. There is a mind-set that's probably pretty common among entrepreneurs, a flexibility: If you hit a wall, back up and adjust your direction. I guess if you run out of adjustments, then you give up. But the dynamics of keeping alive through adaptations gives us an evolutionary advantage. But then, hasn't it always in human history?

In January 2001 the Silicon Valley firm of Compass Venture Partners came through. IBEX was back on track. It now had two new board members, one from Battery, one from Compass, and Jill, still early in the experience, said: "I need them for more than their money. So far they've helped us where we were weak, and their far-reaching resources have made difficulties containable. I have no delusions that I know how to run a company all by myself, but I do have tremendous confidence in my ability to pick the right people to work with and in my ability to learn fast the needed lessons. The right pieces are now in place, and we have

VCs who have knowledge and experience and a track record of honorable conduct and success. So far, so good."

We talked to Jill informally about women entrepreneurs in general, and whether she would encourage them. She responded astutely and compassionately, and in a way that echoed Rebecca MacKinnon: "The best I could do for them is tell them what it is really like. The burden of knowing that others' salaries and families are dependent on your actions. That the time commitment is real and unavoidable. That the stress on the nervous system is real and must be contained somehow. If a woman, knowing the truth about what she is about to undertake, still feels energized, then she doesn't need my encouragement. She has her own."

As Jill looked back over her own experience, the irrepressible and ever-optimistic side of her personality won out:

> Over the past several years, I have used every skill I have. I've learned how to negotiate in difficult situations. I've learned how to control my fear and keep working in the face of adversity. Most of all, over everything else, I'm enjoying the thrill of interacting with smart, talented people. There are few things I've done twice in my life (except have kids and get married), but I expect that because of having built IBEX, I will do something after it that I wouldn't have otherwise. So when you ask if I'd do it all over again, knowing what I know now, I answer that I wouldn't have missed it for anything.

IBEX was going to make it. *Fortune* magazine concurred when it included the company in its 2001 review of the top 100 emerging new companies. But the game was still not won. In fall 2001 the company was due for its next round of financing—the big one that, in its projections, would be the last on the road to profitability and positive cash flow. An e-mail report-cum-exhortation that Jill Card addressed to "Folks" (all IBEX employees) in mid-June 2001 reflected her state of mind. Part of it was to introduce a new vice president of business development, but part of it was the kind of "tough love" that constituted Jill's unique management style. Here are a few extracts:

Folks,

. . .

I will let you know at this point that we are

1) running just on time on Lucent (and that is if we deliver everything from here on out with accuracy and no excuses).
2) going to slide into ST Microelectronics by the skin of our teeth by careful, smart allocation of each person's time to very specific tasks.
3) running above our budgeted expenses because that is life, and there were also some items not included in the budget that should have been. While this is not critical at this time, WE MUST DELIVER THE BETAS ON TIME SO THAT I CAN START THE VENTURE-CAPITAL DANCING by the end of summer. Meantime, I will be ruthless in requiring that no money be spent that can be saved. Eat shit when you travel and sleep in cheap places. Take cheap flights and you will maybe have to come home late or leave early. If we can do all this . . . we will get our funding no sweat and get on with our lives as a real, legitimate and confident company. . . .

Without causing anyone to lose sleep, I need to send a sense of urgency that we continue our tight-knit activities over the next three months. Each of you is here because of your excellence and each of you has given 150% to date. I know it, appreciate it and will not forget it. Please keep it up for a bit longer. I miss my family these days because of the push. And each of us has given up more than a bit of time with our kids and spouses. But this won't last much longer, I promise.

You know that we will make it. G-d knows we've seen FAR more tenuous times and kept the fire going.

※　　※　　※

THE IBM BETA TEST ON THE IBEX DYNAMIC NEURAL CONtroller in Essex Junction, Vermont, held in spring 2001, turned out to be a smash success. So did the tests conducted that summer under the SEMATECH auspices at Lucent and ST Microelectronics. By the fall, IBEX clearly had momentum, and when Jill returned to the Harvard Business School to address the audience at the next New England Springboard in November 2001, it was as a veteran of the venture-capital dance, one who could well say to the new group: "Come on, you can do it too."

6

The Gunslinger

Susan DeFife

IBEX is Jill Card's creation, her struggle, her commitment, and it is hard to imagine her yielding the reins easily. Still, the "exit strategy" is built into any deal an entrepreneur makes with a venture capitalist. "Exit strategy" to a VC means simply "How am I going to get my money out—and when?" It is the great liquidity event all VC deals are based on, when dreams transmogrify into hard cash and the investors get to rake the table clean. In about 70 percent of the successful scenarios, the liquidity event is a sale to another company. The remaining 30 percent go the route of the initial public offering (IPO) or some other form of stock offering. Very often, at such a time, the founding entrepreneur, having made her fortune, is heaped with praise and sent into early, if not always voluntary, retirement.

For all the other things she wants to do in her life, and most certainly could do, it is a stretch right now to imagine Jill Card without IBEX. Or, for that matter, IBEX without Jill Card.

By contrast, I give you Susan DeFife.

※　　※　　※

Susan Williams DeFife was born to be a CEO. A small, thin, attractive blond with a clipped way of talking and an intense gaze, she was raised and educated in Delaware. She decided early on a career in communications, and when the opportunity came her way, she dropped out of college and talked herself into radio and television reporting in Wilmington. From there, she went to work for Delaware governor Mike Castle as a press officer, then went into public relations, then hit the "springboard" that would eventually launch her into her first new-economy venture when she was hired as executive director to a nonprofit called Women Executives in State Government.

There she became interested in what women professionals could accomplish when they joined forces, even in male-dominated fields like American politics. The more she looked, though, the more she came to realize that executive women, women professionals, and women in business as a general group were underserved by the media, particularly by the new media. On-line information focused to a large extent on subjects like child-rearing, homemaking, health and fitness, and pop psychology. The on-line financial and economic worlds were strictly for males.

From the observation came the idea, and from the idea came the vision. In 1994, by then married and the mother of two, De-Fife launched Women's Leadership Connection, a name soon changed to Women's Connection Online when some of her earliest customers complained that they weren't "leaders" but still wanted to subscribe. WCO was offered through Prodigy, the on-line service owned jointly by Sears and IBM, which was then, like AmericaOnline and CompuServe and a number of others, struggling for content, members, and profitability in the fledgling stages of a brand-new medium. Prodigy subscribers paid $9.95 a month. For another $7.00, of which $5.00 went to DeFife, they got the Women's Connection. It was billed as an on-line gathering place for businesswomen, the first of its kind, with bulletin boards, chat rooms, guest experts, news of specific interest, and features on subjects like starting up a new business and raising money in the capital markets.

As DeFife well knew, no new business makes sense in the start-up years. Expenses come first, revenues may be visible down the road, but profits? Profits are somewhere out of sight. For two years, DeFife ran her business in the time-honored, multitasking manner of women entrepreneurs-cum-mothers: "Corporate headquarters" was the sunroom of her house in McLean, Virginia. Supported by her husband—a fair trade, she thought, for having supported him earlier—she painstakingly built WCO to some 4,000 subscribers. At its peak, WCO employed six people, and Susan was finally able to squeeze out a part-time salary for herself—in exchange for a sixty-hour workweek—though the company couldn't really afford it.

This made no sense, none at all. Grow or die, the old business imperative, became an obsession for her, and she wasn't about to die. But in 1996 several things happened that changed her strategy radically.

Out in cyberspace, beyond the on-line services, the World Wide Web had become the new frontier. It had happened virtually overnight. What's more, it was free. As DeFife soon began to hear from her subscribers, nobody wanted to pay for the existing on-line services anymore. Similarly, from the point of view of an Internet business, subscribers and customers could find their way to you on their own, once you had a domain name, a website, and a server to plug you in.

Already, women-oriented sites were springing up like mushrooms. Among the more prominent of these were Women.com, headed by Marleen McDaniel, and, later, iVillage.com, launched with great fanfare and publicity by Nancy Evans and Candice

Carpenter, two ambitious women with access to generous amounts of capital and the conviction that if they made enough noise, they could bully the competition into oblivion and own the market. Both sites would eventually include business-related pages and links, but their objective was to be all things to all women much in the style of the huge-circulation general magazines. For the moment, at least, the business websites continued to be strictly male-oriented, but it was only a matter of time before somebody put together the demographics of women in business and identified the potential in the more targeted audience.

DeFife had come to a personal crossroads. Was she to let WCO go down with the dinosaurs, which is how she perceived the "traditional" subscription-based on-line services? Or was she to take her chances out on the Web?

If the latter, then she realized she couldn't do it slowly. Grow fast or die fast—that became the mantra of everyone who hung out a cyber-shingle in the go-go years of the mid-to-late 1990s. It was like the gold rush: Get out there, stake your claim, and mine it. If you didn't, someone else would. DeFife was also convinced that success on the Internet would require more and better content. Content would be king. If you could build the site with original proprietary material—articles, news stories, interviews, features—then the users, advertisers, and revenues would follow. But content meant staff—editors, technical designers, writers— and staff required capital.

Reluctant as DeFife was at first to approach the capital markets—the combined result, she later said, of her inexperience and the desire she shared with many other women entrepreneurs to keep ownership of her creation for herself and her employees— the time had clearly come to take the plunge. So it was that in

1996, Women's Connection Online became womenCONNECT-.com, and DeFife, with her flair for publicity, set out to create a favorable media buzz about the new Internet company, even as she began to make her first pitches to investors.

One key person (who several years later would become the éminence grise behind our Mid-Atlantic Springboard) was Mario Morino, Washington's preeminent venture capitalist and founder of a nonprofit organization called Netpreneur that sought to foster entrepreneurship in the mid-Atlantic region. Through Netpreneur, DeFife made contact with Esther Smith of the Poretz Group, who later became a member of the women-CONNECT board and introduced Susan right and left to angels and venture capitalists.

Still, money proved hard to raise for the fledgling company. One angel investor who turned DeFife down early was John Burton, managing director of Updata Capital in Reston, Virginia.

"Is this a social cause?" he asked her sardonically when she first pitched him. "Are you asking me for a donation?"

DeFife, undaunted, pursued Burton with revised business plans, one after another rejected, and freshly crunched numbers. He called her "tenacious," even as he turned her down. But tenacity won out, and Burton became the first outside investor with $75,000, which, with later additions, would grow into a 3 percent stake of the company. Yet as DeFife came to realize, his real value to her lay in his pestering and forcing her to focus on the nitty-gritty details that would add up to income-statement and balance-sheet entries.

Investor pressure, by the way, is an experience common to entrepreneurs of all kinds. The value of a really good investor only begins with the signing of the check.

In fall 1996, Susan took on a partner, Gary LaFever, a Washington attorney who had specialized in high-tech companies, start-ups as well as the established, and had been womenCONNECT's lawyer. Between them, they started networking with a vengeance. Gary lent a kind of perceived stability or seriousness to the enterprise, and in April 1997, after some twenty rejections from venture capitalists, they were able to convince Mid-Atlantic Venture Funds to come aboard, to the tune of $500,000 in exchange for a one-third equity ownership. This put a valuation on the company of $1.5 million, not bad for a venture that was less than three years old. More important, the company was finally able to move out of Susan's sunroom into proper office space and begin to make the kind of cash-draining, time-consuming software investments necessary to becoming an Internet player. It could also begin to hire the key staff people it needed, recruiting them over time from *USA Today*, MCI, Nortel, and WorldCom.

The first round of financing—$630,000—would be followed by a second of $1.5 million in 1998, bringing in GE Financial Assurance, Silicon Valley Bank, and Women's Growth Capital Fund as key investors. A third round of $2.1 million came in 1999 from MRW Ventures and Keystone Venture Capital. Susan's stake in the company dropped steadily, to 11 percent of the equity by 2000, with over 50 percent of the shares in the hands of VC investors and almost 20 percent with strategic partners. By that time, though, womenCONNECT was a real company, with a website containing over 4,000 pages.

By the beginning of 2000, womenCONNECT.com (WCC) had formed strategic partnerships with a number of major media companies, including Time Warner/CNN, *USA Today*, Lycos, and CompuServe. CNN, an exclusive for WCC, even held an equity position in the company. WCC's main revenue sources were advertising and e-commerce and product sales through affiliated sites. It captured revenues per 1,000 pageviews—a common industry measurement—at almost six times greater than CBS MarketWatch, four times greater than Women.com, and three times greater than iVillage. It had a click-through to sales ratio at its Amazon.com affiliation of 7–8 percent on diverse products, double the industry average. It had just launched an enVISION channel to help young women in colleges and business schools, now 10 percent of its audience, make the jump into the business world. Its community included 23 percent business owners, 38 percent professional women, and 89 percent college educated. An agreement was being finalized with Sprint PCS to distribute WCC content to six million wireless users, and another was being negotiated with iSyndicate to distribute WCC content throughout a network of 150,000 sites, earning WCC a gross fee of $500–$1,000 per story per feed.

And still, with all this activity, the company found itself on the precipice by mid-2000.

%%%   %%%   %%%

What went wrong?

Well before the dam broke in March, Susan had begun trying to raise her next and fourth round of financing that, per her projections, would be by far her largest but also her last one before profitability. She was looking for funding in the $10–$15 million range. The supporting numbers, unfortunately, called for a leap of faith on the investor's part. The company's revenues had grown from $34,000 in 1997 to $225,000 in 1998 to $481,000 in 1999. For fiscal 2000, a quantum leap was projected to $1.8 million, which presupposed a 1,000 percent increase in advertising revenue. These revenue figures may have been optimistic, DeFife maintained, but they were far from unattainable. Meanwhile, however, costs continued to mushroom, most severely in sales and marketing as Susan and her colleagues strove to reach the critical mass and market penetration that she thought were pre-requisites to profitability. Profitability itself, however, was still several years away. Most of all, WCC's business plan presupposed the healthy continuation of the new-economy boom.

In the meantime, huge influxes of capital had bolstered the few remaining players in the women's-only sector of the Internet. In March 1999, iVillage had made tremendous waves on Wall Street with its IPO. Later, Women.com had gone into a partnership with Hearst, the magazine-publishing giant, absorbing the on-line (and money-losing) editions of *Cosmopolitan, Good House-keeping,* and other Hearst magazines. In fall 1998, Geraldine Laybourne, former CEO of Nickelodeon, had announced a new multimedia women's venture, OxygenMedia, with partnerships that brought in Marcy Carsey and Tom Werner from Carsey-Werner, and Oprah Winfrey. They had not only acquired three websites from AmericaOnline but also planned to launch in 2000 a new women's cable TV channel called Oxygen.

All three of these enterprises were far larger than women-CONNECT and, by comparison, rolling in money. All three, fol-lowing the usual pattern of Internet start-ups, had incurred huge early losses. Individuals may have made huge profits selling iVil-lage stock on or shortly after the IPO, but that was no guarantee of the company's future. Women.com, meanwhile, was obliged in due course to sell out to iVillage, and Oxygen itself had to be boosted by Paul Allen, one of the founders of Microsoft, who doubled his original $100 million stake in the company to $200 million. If the heaviest hitters in the field were nowhere near the break-even point, where did that leave womenCONNECT?

At the heart of the problem was a basic fact of life in the new economy: Everyone loved the Internet, more and more people were getting into it, onto it, and through it, but very few companies had figured out how to make money on it. Many people—from Time Warner executives to Susan DeFife—thought that content was the key, that if you provided great content, people would come. That undoubtedly was true, but there was one major problem: Providing content over the Internet cost money, but Internet consumers expected it to be free. So how did you make money providing content? In theory, you made it the way the portals and search engines such as Yahoo and Ask Jeeves did. These too were free. Their revenues essentially came from each other, either in the form of advertising or in fees in e-commerce sales that came through their links. In one sense, the Internet was a kind of microcosm of the world economy, but it was also a cyberweb in which all the parts were intimately interrelated and interconnected and interdependent through links, "affinities," "strategic partnerships," and connections of one sort or another. The failure of one company was therefore likely to have repercussions far greater and more immediately felt on its neighbors than prevailed in the general economy.

As long as all the companies kept rolling on the yellow brick road to popularity, if not profitability, the boom could go on like a cyber-Ponzi scheme. But if, to be simplistic, dot-com A hit a snag and had to cut its advertising on dot-com B, then dot-com B would fail to make the projections on which its ballooning forecasts relied and would also have to cut its advertising, in which case dot-coms C and D . . .

And so on. All the dominoes would start to tumble.

That is exactly what happened.

At first, as I've noted, Wall Street tried to put a happy face on the event—as well Wall Street might, having been in large part responsible for the ride up. What was happening was just a useful "correction." The last market collapses, it was pointed out, in 1987 and to a lesser degree in 1991–1992, had been equally severe, but the recovery had been sharp, quick, and had zoomed past the precollapse levels within months. Rather than take to the sidelines, frightened investors were counseled to look for opportunities. Buy, buy, buy—this was still Wall Street's advice in April 2000.

But this time, things were different. By the end of the year, when the Nasdaq composite closed at 2,656, it had lost almost half its value in nine months. It would shortly drop below 2,000. But even that steep decline masked the disaster that befell some of the most heavily promoted companies that made up the index. Pundits of one sort or another were now reminded of the 1920s, of tulipmania, of Florida real estate. But probably the best analogy for what happened was the fable about the sardines.

According to the story, a particular shipment of canned sardines went through a number of owners, each buyer becoming a seller, each seller finding a new buyer, until the day when, behind the back of the previous owner of the shipment, the latest buyer opened one of the cans and sampled its contents.

The buyer, it was said, took one mouthful, contorted his face in disgust, and promptly spat out the contents.

"Yuccchhhhhh!" he shouted, running after the seller to protest.

But the seller retorted, "What do you think you're doing? Those sardines aren't for eating. They're for buying and selling."

Too many dot-coms were sardines. They too were for buying and selling.

※ ※ ※

SUSAN DEFIFE FOUND HERSELF SWIMMING UPSTREAM. SHE prospected up and down the network she'd created, searching for funding and coming up empty-handed. Some of womenCON-NECT's existing backers might have been willing to up their share of the ante had she been able to bring new investors to the table, but suddenly there were no new investors, not for a content-based dot-com. She even explored the possibility of a merger with the competition, but the competitive companies were having deep troubles of their own.

With a shocking suddenness, DeFife—like so many others that fateful year—realized she had hit the wall. Conceivably, she could have kept the enterprise running longer by reducing its scale and expenses drastically, but that would have been like putting it on life support. It was pointless. When she put the situation to John Burton, her first and toughest investor—"We're beating a dead horse," she told him—he said, "Shut it down."

Susan kept her colleagues informed every step of the way, and together they kept the website going into summer 2000. She helped every last one of the staff find new jobs (they all did) and made sure there was enough cash left to pay them all, including their accrued vacation pay. That done, on August 31, she sent Bobby Phillips, womenCONNECT's twenty-three-year-old technical director, down to the Exodus Communications building in Herndon, Virginia—he insisted on going alone—and there, amid the racks upon racks of servers for other dot-coms, he quite literally pulled the plug. WomenCONNECT went into liquidation, and that night at a local restaurant the staff held its last party, where Susan, a devout country-and-western fan, recited a great Garth Brooks lyric and responded to it, to general tears and ragged cheers: "I wouldn't have missed this dance for anything in the world."

In her postmortems, DeFife refused to blame the collapse of the Nasdaq, although obviously the timing couldn't have been worse for the company. Rather, there was just too much she didn't know early enough. She blamed herself for having kept the company too small for too long. As good as its acceptance had been, as high as its revenues-per-thousand-pageviews and similar measurements had been, everything had been based on too-small numbers. WomenCONNECT had never reached the critical mass that might have made it not just a good site but an essential one to advertisers, corporate investors, and Wall Street underwriters.

In addition, DeFife admitted, she had been caught up in the fever of the times—the idea that revenues didn't matter and all that counted for a company was the exit strategy that would produce either an IPO or a buyout. Revenues, it turned out, did matter. So did profits. She had been slow, she thought, to explore and maximize every last source of both.

Possibly Susan was right on all counts, but there is another element to be considered as well. It remains to be seen if a stand-alone website for women—*any* website for women—can be a viable commercial enterprise. The emphasis should be on *stand-alone*. More and more, as our experience with the Internet grows, I think it's becoming clearer that successful large-scale stand-alone sites will be few and far between. Will Amazon.com make it? The verdict, as of this writing, is still out. The verdict is also still out on the surviving women-oriented sites. My feeling is that Oxygen has a better chance than iVillage because it is tied into a cable TV operation. On the other hand, iVillage has common ownership now with Lifetime, through Hearst's investment, and access to a significant list of women's magazines including *Harper's Bazaar, Cosmopolitan, Marie Claire,* and others. Despite the huge losses incurred in the 1990s by the major media who tried, however clumsily, to push their way onto the Internet, I do think media companies that are firmly established elsewhere, as broadcasters or print providers, will in time find their way back onto the Internet—and operate profitably.

But that is for the future. To come back to Susan DeFife, she herself viewed her six years with womenCONNECT.com as a learning experience, not as proof of her inadequacy. She may have cost her investors a grand total of $5.5 million, but every last one of them spoke highly of her, and many said they would gladly invest in her again if she ever became involved in the right business. Whereas many women, unlike their male counterparts, take failure in business personally and as prima facie proof of their inadequacy, Susan looked on it as a kind of badge of honor and as a rite of passage.

Most remarkable, a scant thirty-six days after the demise of womenCONNECT, Susan DeFife was back as the CEO of a year-old company, gearing up for a major fund-raising effort on its behalf.

%%%   %%%   %%%

DEFIFE HAD SEVERAL JOB INTERVIEWS THAT SUMMER AND met with headhunters, only to decide that her heart wasn't in a corporate setting or even in working for anyone else. She had the fever. She wanted to be a CEO, and like a prizefighter who's been knocked through the ropes, she wanted back in the ring as fast as possible.

Her chance came from an unexpected source.

Albert Gidari had been named the first "entrepreneur-in-residence" at the Seattle-based law firm of Perkins Coie, which specialized in representing high-tech companies. Gidari had previously served as CEO of an Internet bank and financial services company and had founded G-Savvy.com, an accelerator for emerging companies. He and Susan knew each other because both sat on a George Mason University board, George Mason being the home of the Capitol Connection broadcasting system. But when Gidari first called her about HearingRoom, she was less than overwhelmed.

HearingRoom was a fledgling company that transmitted near-real-time streaming-text transcripts of congressional hearings over the Internet in conjunction with linked audio of the same material. In other words, it allowed subscribers to both read and hear what had just transpired in Congress's hearing rooms. Furthermore, it stored the transmissions in a database that could be accessed and researched by a keyword system.

The company's revenue model called for paid-in-advance, declining-balance subscriptions. For an additional fee, subscribers—which by the end of 2000 would include General Motors, Boeing, Hill and Knowlton, and the National Institutes of Health—could choose in advance the hearings they wanted covered, and when (real-time or next-day) they wanted delivery. By the time Al Gidari approached Susan DeFife about the company, almost all the hearing rooms of the Capitol had been wired, and all the public hearings conducted by House and Senate committees were available to subscribers. The company planned to begin providing selected coverage of executive-branch hearings in 2001.

HearingRoom had revenues—some $200,000 in just the few months since its launch in June 2000—and parts of its technology were proprietary. To counter annoying inaccuracies of voice-recognition technology, HearingRoom had worked with specialists in audio and text streaming, speech recognition, and—most important—"voice writing." A voice writer is like a simultaneous translator, a person skilled in dictating speech he or she has just heard into a specialized microphone. With the aid of voice-recognition software, voice writers were able to transcribe accurately the many voices of a congressional committee room into streaming text for the Internet with only a brief delay in real-time transmission.

At first glance, the company looked to DeFife like a good but limited niche business. Philip Angell and Christopher Chapin, two of the founders, had built a subscription base that could be expanded, but they had the Washington connections to do this. Angell had been head of corporate communications for Browning Ferris and Monsanto, two Fortune 500 companies, and also chief of staff to the administrator of the Environmental Protection Agency. Chapin had been consultant and partner with the management consultant firms of Booz, Allen, and Hamilton and the MAC Group. Angell had raised $850,000 in seed money for the launch, had won permission to wire the Senate and House committee rooms, and clearly had a good sense of publicity. The *New York Times* and the *Washington Post* had covered the company at its opening, and a major article would appear in the November issue of *Wired* magazine.

As useful as HearingRoom was to the Beltway world, though,

in and of itself it had limited business potential. So why did Angell and his backers want a new CEO? And why DeFife?

The answer lay in the business plan. It was sixty pages long, extremely well put together, and identified other applications for HearingRoom's technology in industries that had nothing to do with the nation's capital.

A key characteristic of successful entrepreneurs is the ability to seize an unexpected opportunity and run with it. Shortly after she'd read the business plan, DeFife met Angell for breakfast at a Washington hotel. As she later recalled, he was visionary, persuasive, and "passionate about what the technology could do." He'd already been exploring other applications and opportunities, particularly one in the financial community that would ultimately be named AnalystsCall. But these new ventures would require expanded contacts, a much expanded sales and marketing team, and eventually a technical support staff far more ambitious than what was needed for HearingRoom. All these, in turn, would require two things: professional management and an influx of new capital. Angell needed a new CEO to operate an expanding business and to find and deal with new investors.

DeFife quickly sounded out technology people she knew. The more she heard, the more intrigued she became. The business was clearly fundable, she thought, and she saw strong exit possibilities. She liked Angell too, and she particularly liked the potential on the AnalystsCall side. There she saw a once-in-a-lifetime opportunity.

A new regulation of the Securities and Exchange Commission was just about to go into effect, putting an end to an old and unfair Wall Street practice. Traditionally, publicly traded corporations made their quarterly-earnings calls to only a limited audience of stock-market analysts at the big brokerage houses.

This system perpetuated a form of insider access that the SEC had been created to stamp out, and the commission's answer came finally in the form of Regulation FD, effective October 23, 2000, which required publicly held companies to make broadly available to the general public and the media all material information that could affect investor decisions and to do so at the same time as they informed industry analysts. Quarterly-earnings calls now had to be made immediately public, and the method the vast majority of companies chose in order to comply was an audio webcast over the Internet.

The opportunity for AnalystsCall was obvious. Analysts, journalists, investors, and countless others for whom timely financial information was critical would be able not only to hear the webcast but also to receive it in streaming text, to copy it, and to have the material available in a database, in both text and audio, with keyword capability. Selected elements of the webcast could now be available, through the AnalystsCall service, with just a few clicks of the mouse. The only existing alternative for the financial services firms was to use their own stenographers to create stand-alone transcripts—at slow speed and high cost and without search or index features.

As DeFife discovered, there were several services outstanding that already streamed the audio of corporate calls to analysts— Yahoo Finance, for one—but none offered near-real-time transcripts. A service called PRNewswire maintained an archive of events it covered, and the Investor Broadcast Network provided selected transcripts within a day or two after the call had been made. But no one offered the timeliness and synchronicity of AnalystsCall.

There were other applications for the technology that had scarcely been explored. One involved the music industry. Another was e-learning, one of the fastest-growing markets on the Internet. In addition, custom packages could easily be developed, either on a turnkey or licensing basis. The oral content of sales meetings, training classes, and conferences—to cite a few possibilities—could easily be converted into text for almost-immediate use and indexed and archived for future search and recall. The larger and more geographically diverse the client company, the more valuable the services.

From Susan's point of view, the company had a great idea, a technology that was proprietary in part and had already been tested in its HearingRoom applications, and a brand-new, large, and deep-pocketed marketplace. Although there was nothing to prevent heavy hitters in the financial-information field from inventing their own forms of streaming text and archival database, Angell's company had a clear competitive edge. It had to expand, test, market, sell—to "ramp up" as it is said in the Internet world—and it needed to do so at Internet speed.

Even in tough times, the situation was made to order for venture-capital investing.

Made to order too for Susan DeFife.

※ ※ ※

THIRTY-SIX DAYS AFTER THE DEMISE OF WOMEN CONNECT, DeFife signed on as CEO of StreamingText, the new name of the company. She had an equity position, offices in Washington, D.C., as well as at company headquarters in Reston, Virginia, and a mandate to fulfill the vision she now shared with Angell, Chapin, and the company's director of technology, Jake Levine. In the immediate future, the company had hiring to do, field testing to push forward, new customers to solicit and sell, and, above all, funds to raise.

One of DeFife's first acts as CEO was to file an application for the Springboard forum to be held in New York in March 2001. She did so, she admitted later, not because she felt she needed help or coaching as a presenter—in this, also by her later admission, she turned out to be wrong—but in order to gain entrée to New York investors. Through her womenCONNECT experience, and having already presented at the Mid-Atlantic Venture Association, she felt reasonably well acquainted with the venture-capital scene in and around Washington. While she would be pursuing investors there—and her colleagues had already started—she had a sense that VCs in New York (which was, after all, the financial capital of the world) would find StreamingText intriguing. She had a couple of good contacts, but she needed more, and so, long before Springboard, for which notification of acceptance wouldn't come until late in the year, she found herself shuttling north at least once a week for meetings and networking.

Networking, networking, networking.

One of Susan's first contacts in New York was Lisa Caputo, whom she knew from Caputo's work on women's issues in the Clinton White House. Caputo had since gone on to Citicorp, where she started "Women & Co.," an initiative to attract high-net-worth women as customers to the bank. Caputo passed the StreamingText business plan on to her venture group. Streaming-Text was still too young and the numbers too small to appeal to the venture-group investors, but one of them put in a call to a friend at Reuters, the British news service and financial-information giant, with headquarters now in New York. The friend at Reuters wasn't interested in StreamingText as a possible acquisition or investment, but she too was intrigued by the promise of the technology and referred DeFife to Betty Wong, U.S. equities editor for Reuters. Back to New York went DeFife and Angell to give a demonstration on how their product worked. Wong and her colleagues were much taken with it and agreed to test it with a few upcoming analysts' calls. In short order, Reuters became a StreamingText subscriber.

Meanwhile, Philip Angell had been working with an editor at Dow Jones, Reuters's number-one competitor. Even before De-Fife joined the company, he had demonstrated the technology for Dow, and the company had committed to test it. The tests went extremely well, and one of DeFife's first tasks as CEO was to negotiate the Dow Jones subscriber contract.

Neither Reuters nor Dow had ever heard of StreamingText before Angell and DeFife set their sights on them, but one thing had led to another, and for DeFife to take the floor at Springboard in March with the two contracts in her pocket gave StreamingText a terrific leg up in appealing to venture capitalists.

These weren't the only developments. DeFife had commitments from two new employees to fill the key positions of chief operating officer and vice president for sales. The company had begun to sell custom packages to major corporations, and these would include Motorola, KEA Capital, Allied Waste Management, and Monsanto. Finally, through networking in a different direction, serious conversations were already in progress with several potential investors and/or strategic partners. Among them were the Thomson Financial Network, NewsAlert, and a privately owned, Canadian-based company called Syoni. Syoni was already offering purely audio versions of analysts' calls for some 5,000 customers.

DeFife took the floor in second position at the March New York Springboard, held at Chase Manhattan Plaza in the heart of the financial district. As she walked onto the stage and launched into her pitch, I marveled at how professional she was. If I hadn't known, I never would have guessed that seven months before, she'd had to pull the plug on a venture into which she'd put six years of heart and soul. To call that "a learning experience" would be to minimize the pain and the effort that had gone into womenCONNECT. But DeFife *had* learned, and with every crisp and confident moment of her presentation, I thought how much of an asset she was to Springboard, just as Springboard was to her.

※   ※   ※

BUT THE STORY ISN'T OVER. DeFife and Angell had presented at the Springboard forum looking for $3 million, but they revised their numbers downward because of the tight capital marketplace, seeking $1 million immediately and another $3 million at the end of 2001. With the revised numbers, they got quick interest from a North Carolina investment group and promptly moved on to due diligence, which StreamingText would pass.

Meanwhile, however, negotiations were also proceeding with the Canadian company, Syoni, for a possible merger that would marry StreamingText's differentiating technology with Syoni's extensive customer base. One scenario involved setting up a new company that would acquire both companies. Another was a straight stock swap. When the North Carolinians, with Southern grace, heard of the impending merger, they were happy enough to step aside and wait, still greatly interested, they said, in an eventual investment in the combined entity.

But "the dance," to use Jill Card's term, didn't end here either. Another potential acquirer—of both companies—emerged like a leviathan from the depths. This one was a "strategic investor," that is, a large company already active in the field of financial information and interested in building its ongoing business through the Syoni-StreamingText combination. In initial conversations, these new people wanted to become lead investor in the new round of financing, with an option to buy all the outstanding stock of the two companies later, but in the end, negotiations led to a straight acquisition.

In the context of the tough business climate at the end of 2001, the deal satisfied all parties. By mutual agreement, the details of the deal cannot be disclosed here, but the acquiring company is getting a very useful and potentially very profitable add-on to the services it already provides, and all but one of the StreamingText-Syoni principals will stay with the new company.

The one exception? The one who is leaving the combined company?

Susan DeFife.

As is so often the case in corporate acquisitions, there is no room in the management layers of the new enterprise for the leader of the old. Susan is similarly bound not to disclose the terms of her buyout package, but when she reported it in a phone conversation, the irrepressible lilt in her voice suggested that she'd done very well.

"Besides," she said, "I'm free now."

Free to do what?

"Well, free to find another start-up. Do it all over again. After all, isn't that what gunslingers do?"

7

The Brave New World

of Biotech

Jane Homan

It's a long way from dot-coms to pigs, longer still from neural networks and semiconductors to retrovectors and an experimental farm outside of Sauk City, Wisconsin.

Biotech.

Perhaps more than any other sector of the knowledge industries, companies in biotechnology are ideal candidates for venture-capital investment. Most of them are based on proprietary discoveries made in the scientific laboratory, and for those that succeed, the payoffs can be enormous. A great many, such as the one I am about to describe, have spun off from universities and pay royalties to the particular university where the research was performed. Indeed, the whole subject of the commercialization of academic research has become highly controversial— Who should own a discovery? Who should profit from it?—but at least in the sciences, the days of the ivory tower are long gone.

Biotech has benefited from the cross-pollination of the university lab and business office. The industry has also proved hospitable to women, and one of my favorite venture capitalists who traffics in the knowledge industries, Pat Cloherty, claims that virtually every new biotech company she considers for investment has one or more women on its senior management team. Still, women in biotech trying to raise capital for their fledgling companies face the same problems all women entrepreneurs do, as well as some peculiar to their field. They've been represented at all the Springboard forums.

THE FIRST TIME I SAW JANE HOMAN WAS WHEN SHE WALKED onto the stage at Springboard Midwest in May 2001 on the Northwestern campus in Evanston, Illinois. She had come to represent a brand-new company, ioGenetics, which was a spin-off of another company called Gala Design. The two companies had been founded by the same scientific team and had the same revolutionary—and proprietary—technology at their heart. But Gala Design, now five years old, used the technology to produce biopharmaceutical proteins in cell culture and in the milk of cows. The scalability of its technology—that is, how quickly and easily it could be brought to high levels of production—and its relative low cost had made it possible to manufacture recombinant, or genetically engineered, protein drugs for much larger patient populations than was currently feasible by other methods. Gala had begun to position itself as the market leader in protein expression, which meant practically that its potential customers included every biopharmaceutical company in the world. It had staffed up, it was well financed, and its road to high profitability was wide open.

Enter ioGenetics.

The new ioGenetics company used the same gene-transfer technology developed at Gala Design to produce "transgenic" livestock. Its animals would carry gene insertions that were stable and transmit them consistently to their offspring. As its business plan stated directly, the fledgling company had "the potential to dramatically enhance the performance and profitability of swine, dairy and beef herds throughout the United States and internationally." If ioGenetics succeeded, it would be opening the doors wide to the brave new world of genetically engineered animal agriculture.

The composed, handsome, and self-assured woman who now stood on our Springboard stage was Dr. Jane Homan, CEO of io-Genetics. She had just a trace of a British accent. Born in Maidstone, England, she had grown up in Scotland where her father wanted her to study classics and law. Instead, she pursued a degree in veterinary medicine from the University of Glasgow. After that, she struck out for the Canadian prairies and north woods and, as she wryly put it, "I guess I forgot to go home." She earned her master's in diagnostic veterinary microbiology at the University of Saskatchewan in Canada in 1977, then her Ph.D. in veterinary virology at the University of Wisconsin–Madison in 1980.

In the 1980s and well into the 1990s, while an assistant professor first at Washington State, then back again at Wisconsin, Dr. Jane was all over the Western Hemisphere and Africa on a variety of assignments and projects. She worked on multiple epidemiological field studies in South America, including the equine encephalitis virus, in the early 1980s. She did livestock development in Gambia for USAID in 1986 and 1987. From 1991 to 1993, as a consultant to the United Nations Food and Agricultural Organization, she was involved in training and implementing a computerized management information system for a model integrated dairy development program in Ecuador. She published widely in her field, gave seminars, found time for symposia and conferences. Then, in 1992, back at the University of Wisconsin, she was named director of its Babcock Institute for International Dairy Research and Development.

Along the way, Dr. Jane met Dr. Robert Bremel, initially as a colleague on a university-sponsored trip. He would become her husband, then her business partner. Born and raised on his family's dairy farm in western Wisconsin, a full professor at Wisconsin–Madison (now its youngest professor emeritus), Bob Bremel had managed a large mammary physiology research lab for many years, and it was his work in biochemistry and molecular biology, as they related to milk production, that formed the techno-scientific underpinning of the company they founded together, Gala Design.

Jane didn't mention their life together during her presentation, but their professional relationship had clearly worked to perfection. "We tend to have breakfast-time conversations about things like global food security and epidemiology," Jane told me afterward. Bob Bremel may have masterminded the scientific discoveries that led to Gala Design's breakthrough and technological edge, but Jane Homan brought considerable management and organizational experience to the partnership. As she later explained it, "I remember, on meeting Bob and accusing him of being a 'gene jockey,' his commenting that molecular biology wasn't difficult. 'You just have to think like a molecule,' he said. Definitely weird. No doubt about it, he's the dreamer. I'm the organizer and driver."

※　※　※

THE SCIENTIFIC CONCEPT ON WHICH BOTH GALA DESIGN and ioGenetics rely—the use of so-called retrovectors to deliver genetic material into cells—dates back to the early 1970s and the myriad discoveries concerning the nature and manipulation of DNA and RNA. Much of that work came about through the still earlier studies of the Nobel Prize–winning microbiologist Joshua Lederberg and subsequently the late Howard Temin and David Baltimore, both Nobel laureates-to-be. Both Lederberg and Temin were at the University of Wisconsin.

Temin and Baltimore discovered that strange and tiny microbe known as the retrovirus, named for its unique ability to transform reverse mirror images of its RNA to produce a DNA version of its genes and then to insert itself into the genetic material of a host's cells. The retrovirus was first linked to certain types of cancer, then to HIV and AIDS. Consequently, it was intensely studied, and some of the researchers—Dr. Temin among them—had the idea of putting this natural enemy to good use.

Medical history abounds in such examples. After all, the smallpox vaccine we still use is actually a cowpox derivative discovered by Dr. Edward Jenner in eighteenth-century England. And it was a fungus mold, penicillium, growing on decaying fruit that became the first of our wonder drugs, thanks to the discoveries of Sir Alexander Fleming and others in 1928.

In the case of retroviruses, it was Bob Bremel's laboratory at Wisconsin, building on Temin's work and collaborating with researchers at the University of California at San Diego, that explored and developed the retrovector concept. The scientists gutted the viruses to remove their ability to replicate and rebuilt them to carry synthetic genes. The viruses thus became vectors, or delivery agents, for transmitting genes into living organisms. Later, the scientists figured out how to use such vectors in very small numbers to deliver a cargo, or "payload," of genes to the oocytes (the eggs) of farm animals prior to fertilization. Almost 100 percent of the embryos resulting from the fertilization process then carried the gene in question. In terms of accuracy, the Wisconsin method far surpassed any of the competing technologies available for transgenic work. In other words, as often occurs in emerging technologies, it leapfrogged the first-generation science of transgenesis, which had produced the first transgenic animals in the early 1980s. A number of start-up companies had been struggling ever since, with often frustrating results, to bring biopharmaceutical products produced in transgenic animals to clinical trials.

Gala Design was founded in 1996. Its funding, in seed and first-round financing over the next three years, amounted to just under $5 million, obtained from private investors and from Venture Investors Early Stage Fund II, a venture-capital group in Madison. Bremel and Homan had protected their work with patents and trademarks, and they had exclusive licensing, on a royalty basis, of the parts owned by the University of Wisconsin. In 1998 they published the results of their research and described their new Transgametic technology. By this time, of course, another highly publicized event of huge and dramatic impact to science and to commerce was well on its way: the sequencing of the human genome and the completion of the Human Genome Project. The Gala Design business plan (written by Jane Homan) described one of its effects as follows:

> To benefit from genomics and The Human Genome Project, biopharmaceutical companies have begun to focus on expression of the proteins encoded by the thousands of genes that have been sequenced. The magnitude of this challenge represents a significant opportunity for Gala. There may be as many as 4 to 10 times as many unique proteins as there are genes identified. . . . Gala will apply its technology to express the proteins from the genes to help biopharmaceutical companies screen and identify drug targets and to manufacture proteins that have pharmaceutical value.

The speed with which Gala's technology permits evaluation and a seamless scale up to manufacturing provides us a unique competitive advantage. Proteins such as antibodies, enzymes, hormones and immunomodulators will potentially be exciting new treatments for common diseases such as Alzheimer's disease, cancer, Parkinson's disease and diabetes.

One key to Gala's potential was its ability to make small quantities (micrograms) of a complex recombinant protein for research and then scale up its production in progressively larger quantities, all the way up to commercial manufacture in metric tons. By the time of our Springboard Midwest forum, it had won competitive grants and commercial protein production contracts. It had a staff of thirty, including eight Ph.D. scientists, had leased and operated a dairy farm dedicated to its projects, and was well on its way toward profitability.

※　※　※

EVEN THOUGH THE TECHNOLOGICAL BASE WAS THE SAME, and even though the founders and the labs and the farm were the same, ioGenetics took Jane Homan and her husband into controversial territory. The mere mention of "genetic engineering" today conjures up images of street protests and stories about Europeans refusing to buy American beef and the fate of monarch butterflies at their migratory stopovers in the cornfields of the Midwest. Many of these concerns are legitimate and deserving of study. And they are being studied. But anxiety persists.

Genetic engineering, it should be noted, is nothing new. Neolithic farmers, as archaeologists have discovered, experimented in hybridization and breeding of both crops and domestic animals more than 10,000 years ago. Everything we've eaten since—from cultivated corn to herds of "purebred" beef cattle—has been "engineered" by generations of farmers seeking to improve their yields and their revenues. Prize bulls were mated with prize cows, peaches were crossed with plums to produce nectarines, and so forth. In the main, our efforts to improve crops and animals have benefited us and are today a necessity to keep our growing world population from widespread famine.

So why all the clamor? To a degree, it's the fault of the agribusiness giants who, by their arrogance and secrecy and, in some cases, their negligence, have created an atmosphere of deep suspicion among us. But even more, even without specific cause, we're simply afraid. Afraid that technology is progressing too fast. Afraid that we're no longer in control and that, in tampering with nature, we're playing God. The deep moral conflicts in our society—over abortion, for instance, over stem-cell research involving human embryos, over cloning—all reflect the same anxiety: that we may be doing something terrible and irrevocable to ourselves and our planet. Science and technology, some of us fear, have run amok.

Science fiction mirrors it too. As creator of the Sci-Fi Channel, I've always admired the imagination of science-fiction writers and their ability to grasp what the future could bring. Ever since Mary Shelley's *Frankenstein,* sci-fi writers have been warning us about what could happen when scientists got carried away. Remember H. G. Wells's *The Island of Dr. Moreau*? E. M. Forster's *The Machine Stopped*? Robert Louis Stevenson's *Dr. Jekyll and Mr. Hyde*? All troubling tales of scientific manipulation.

When I was growing up, the great scare was nuclear winter—a real enough menace. Today's equivalents are probably global warming and Dolly, the cloned sheep. All of these were, and are, man-made dangers, and we have to summon the intelligence and the will to deal with them. But along the way, science and technology have gotten a bad rap.

Mindful of this, and of the disastrous consequences that ensued for major biotech corporations when they failed to take these issues seriously and confront them openly, Jane Homan wrote a kind of manifesto for her fledgling company:

> With the experience of crop transgenics in mind, ioGenetics will move proactively to make sure the positive benefits of enhanced livestock genetics are communicated to consumers. The process of regulatory approval will be conducted with transparency. As ioGenetics hires senior management staff, the ability to operate and communicate in this environment will be a key qualification. IoGenetics plans to establish an advisory "sounding board" which can help keep it alert and sensitive to the concerns of consumer groups and the general public. . . .
>
> As pioneers in the field, we have the road open ahead of us. We need to make sure we both talk and walk the high road of animal welfare, respect of consumer concerns, and regulatory openness. We recognize that the need to listen is as important as that of communicating our own goals.

This statement of intent may sound visionary and brave, but it has already had practical consequences. Jane knew in advance that regulatory approval would be the cornerstone of the new company's success—and a potential pitfall. In 1999, even before ioGenetics was spun out as a company, Jane and her colleagues opened dialogues with an alphabet soup of government regulatory agencies, including the FDA (Food and Drug Administration), the USDA APHIS (United States Department of Agriculture—Animal Plant Health Inspection Service), and FSIS (Food Safety Inspection Service). Somewhat to her surprise—she said she'd half expected a group of tired old fogies—she found the FDA people smart, extremely well-informed, and most helpful and open to discussion. They made it clear that the approval paths for ioGenetics products would be complicated but navigable. Some of the products might be classified as animal drugs, others as food additives. Some would require target animal safety data collection, field trial data collection, and environmental impact studies. But at the same time, the FDA fully understood the potential benefits of the ioGenetics technology—for example, in bringing about a reduction in the use of antibiotics by raising disease-resistant animal herds.

The regulatory process didn't end with these meetings either. The Animal Welfare Act requires oversight by an Institutional Animal Care and Welfare Committee, and certain NIH (National Institutes of Health) guidelines come into play if the company wants to be eligible for federal funding. Furthermore, severe NIH guidelines on biosafety kick in the moment a company starts to work with vectors and recombinant DNA.

%%   %%   %%

THE BUSINESS MODEL OF THE BIOTECH START-UP, AS I'VE mentioned, is in many respects perfect for venture capital, but not all venture capitalists are comfortable investing in the field. For one thing, biotech entrepreneurs are almost all scientists. Typically, they have grown up as professionals in academic or, in some cases, government research laboratories, and that's the "language" they speak. Often at the core of their business, as in the case of ioGenetics, lies a proprietary element developed in their former job, the patent of which is frequently co-owned by the entrepreneur-to-be and his or her former research institution. The exploitation of the patented knowledge often requires payment of a royalty. The networking that links biotech entrepreneurs and venture capitalists most often evolves out of their contacts within the scientific community. This doesn't mean that all venture capitalists who invest in biotech companies must have a Ph.D. in genetics or biochemistry, but if they don't, there should be colleagues or close advisers who do.

Another characteristic of biotech start-ups is the longer time lag compared with companies in other fields. At least in boom times, venture capitalists are used to dealing in a three- to five-year plan from investment to profitability and exit strategy. But the ioGenetics technology application, for instance, depends on breeding animals, like cows, that have a nine-month gestation period, meaning that the development of traits, or phenotypes, and their genetic establishment in subsequent generations take time. And as anybody can attest who has ever been involved in the field trials required by government regulators, the path to approval can take years.

The business model for ioGenetics is based on the development and commercialization of many genetic traits. Some of these are so-called input traits, meaning that they will primarily benefit livestock producers by reducing their costs and/or increasing their productivity. For instance, ioGenetics has identified specific, economically important animal-population diseases and transgenetic approaches to building resistance to them. One of these, BLV, or bovine leukemia virus, has been found in approximately 30 percent of dairy cattle in 90 percent of American herds. The young ioGenetics has a project well under way to create transgenic cattle resistant to the disease, and at the time of Homan's presentation at Springboard, it was showing remarkable progress.

Other traits are so-called output traits, new genetic characteristics in animals driven by the needs of food processors, food retailers, and/or consumers. In the case of dairy cattle, the ioGenetics technology can increase the content of naturally occurring proteins, can add new components to milk, or can change the characteristics of existing components. Similarly, genetic controls can curtail the use of antibiotics in animal food, and genetic blocks to endo- and ectoparasites can reduce pesticide usage.

In Jane Homan's forecast, though, net income wouldn't move into the black until the fifth year of operations, while the great burst into high profitability wouldn't come until year seven. But the promise is real if the previously developed market for transgenic crops is taken as a guide. As Jane has pointed out, two-thirds of the soybeans planted in the United States in 2001 carried a Round-up Ready R trait, licensed from Monsanto. The value of this single plant trait in royalties in the United States alone was estimated to be over $500 million. Based on this model, Jane projected in year ten of the ioGenetics plan a revenue stream approaching $1 billion.

Inevitably, with such a huge potential market, ioGenetics faces competing technologies. "Pronuclear microinjection," which injects several hundred copies of DNA into an embryo, has been in use for more than a decade, but its inefficiency—only 1 percent of embryos are fertilized—has made the cost of creating founder animals by this method insupportably high. "Nuclear transfer"—popularly known as cloning—has four strikes against it, not the least of which is that it stops genetic progress by simply copying what was, rather than allowing genetic gain to pursue its natural course. It thereby removes genetic diversity from the agricultural process, and widespread cloning in the United States would only exacerbate the already existent problem of too much inbreeding.

Of paramount importance to the biotech start-up is the management team. The group at ioGenetics is loaded with scientists, of course, but scientists with a business slant. Dr. Thomas Howard, hired in 2000 to head Gala Design's regulatory affairs and now performing the same function at ioGenetics, was a veterinarian trained in virology who had previously served as administrator of the Wisconsin Division of Animal Health (state veterinarian) and had already led the process of bringing Gala Design's operations into compliance with the FDA and other regulatory agencies. Michi Imboden, an immunologist, joined the ioGenetics team from the University of Wisconsin Clinical Cancer Center. The chairman of Gala Design's board of directors and a board member of ioGenetics was Thomas McNally, formerly president of two different divisions of Abbott Laboratories, who brought corporate savvy, a wide network of contacts, and broad experience in the agricultural products markets.

But at the core of the team remained the husband-and-wife partnership, Bob Bremel and Jane Homan, who, in Jane's words, "didn't set out to make a company to make money, but because we needed a company to reach the scientific goals that couldn't be realized operating inside a university." Once they realized there was money to be made, first with Gala Design, then with ioGenetics, they also realized they didn't want to be spectators at what was going to develop from their ideas. So a pair of scientists from academia became entrepreneurs and, in a few short years, businesspeople of high caliber.

%%   %%   %%

ONE UNFORTUNATE ASPECT OF WRITING A BOOK "FROM THE front lines" is that the author is compelled to leave a story in midstream. I'm eagerly awaiting news of what happens to Jane Homan and ioGenetics. Overall, the business plan called for a total capitalization of $15–$20 million from a combination of venture funds and strategic partners, $3.5 million of it needed soon.

Despite the tough times of the moment, including the economic uncertainties of 2001 exacerbated by the terrorist attacks of September 11, I don't see how the company can fail. The promise—what Jane Homan called "a tollgate to the future"—strikes me as irresistible to venture capitalists, although Jane believes that in today's difficult climate, the short-term support she needs may be more likely to come from individual investors than venture-capitalist groups. She and Bob Bremel are following a prudent, watch-and-wait course—"a smolder rather than a burn rate," as she puts it—but they also are moving forward with their plans. Wearing their Gala Design hats, they presented in October 2001 at the BIO Venture Fair at the Washington, D.C., Hilton, a new forum sponsored by the biotech industry organization that, I am delighted to say, seems to have borrowed elements from Springboard, including a preliminary boot camp for participants. Despite the timing—just a few weeks after the attacks on the World Trade Center and the Pentagon—the fair was extremely well attended, the atmosphere upbeat, and Jane went home from it feeling not only that biotech is alive and well but that we, as an economy, have bottomed and are at the beginning of a long, slow upswing in investment activity.

May she prove to be right. And may her story be an inspiration to other women scientists who are doing the research today that will lead to the creation of the biotech start-ups of tomorrow.

Meanwhile, Gala Design marches on. As I write, the company is nearing completion on the construction of a new 44,000-square-foot facility. Guess who the project coordinator is, presumably wearing her hard hat?

None other than Dr. Jane Homan.

8

Doing It

We learn by doing and by listening to others who have done it.

Immediately after the Silicon Valley Springboard of January 2000, we encouraged our entrepreneurs to critique the event. Many of them would have wanted an early, and complete, explanation of all that would be expected of them. The coaches had been great, they said, but idiosyncratic too. Where was the overview? The road map?

Our answer evolved into a daylong session we called "Boot Camp," in which our chosen finalists assembled for the first time and heard in detail what was in store for them. But their question—Where is the road map?—and our answers are just as valid for you, the reader. The stories you have just read exemplify how women entrepreneurs in totally unrelated fields have driven their companies from the original "light bulb" forward. The following chapters lay out in concrete form the guidelines any successful entrepreneur must follow on the journey to success (see Figure 8.1).

The "light bulb" is your fundamental idea. It answers the question, What problem do you and your product solve? Your product need not be revolutionary; products that revolutionize an industry are rare. After all, Michael Dell didn't invent the PC, and Microsoft's fabulous success was based on software it originally bought from other innovators. But your company's products or services must fill a gap or need in the marketplace. You must of-

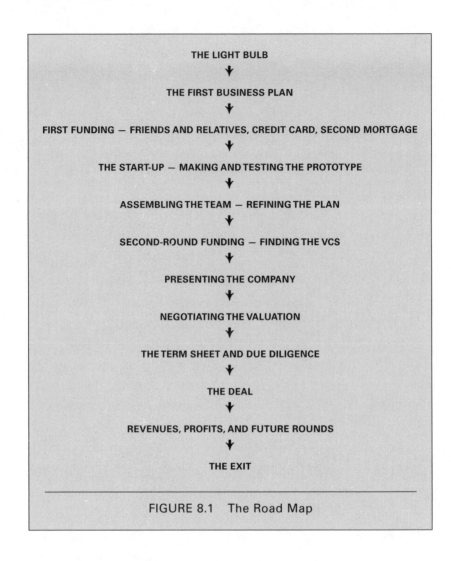

FIGURE 8.1   The Road Map

fer a solution to a problem that your competitors don't or offer it at a cost no one else can match.

In other words, you need a competitive edge.

Obviously, investors respond favorably to proprietary products that can be protected either through patent or copyright, but they have also learned to be cautious about the risk of still newer technologies that might render yours obsolete overnight. Therefore you—and your presentation, oral or written, when you get to it—must establish quickly and convincingly what your product does, what differentiates it from its competition, how big the overall market for it is, and how "scalable" it is.

As I've indicated, "scalability" must be part of your vocabulary, for it is a buzzword in business schools and investment circles. It simply means how fast and how economically you can get from "here" to "there." "Here" is presumably where you are now, right at the beginning: for example, at the prototype stage, in alpha or beta testing, or in distribution to a limited market. "There" is where your business plan says you are headed: the full, big, and profitable market you envision.

Scalability, as already mentioned, is paramount to venture capitalists because of the obsolescence factor. Looming over a great many new-economy enterprises is the specter of some brand-new, unexpected technological innovation that will leapfrog their patents and copyrights and leave them rudderless, moribund, like abandoned ghost ships. Consider one recent example: all the investors' money that went swirling into the cyberseas in the 1990s when the CD-ROM, as an informational tool, was rendered largely obsolete by the Internet.

Hand in hand with scalability come questions of pricing. Can your customers afford the products or services you are going to offer them? How do you plan to convince them of the savings and value-addeds that will be theirs? If you must price at a loss going in—and many businesses have to in order to establish themselves—at what volume will you reach profitability, and how long will it take you?

Already you are beyond the light bulb stage and into questions that must be answered, even when you're raising your first funds.

Unless you are a nonprofit, these are the kinds of nitty-gritty commercial issues you must be addressing in any business plan or presentation. Obviously, in a formal business plan, they must be supported by financial numbers and forecasts, but you should be capable of analyzing them on your own in the give-and-take of conversation as well as in the formal passages you are going to write.

To put it another way, your business plan—the document articulating where your company has been and where it is going in words and numbers—is every bit as important to raising funding as is your idea itself. You should be writing the plan early and revising it constantly in the light of developments. The financial community is accustomed to business plans with a particular content organized in a particular structure. There are books and workbooks and websites on the Internet that give instructions and tips, so you should have no trouble getting started. But there are issues we stress at Springboard that are worth the review even of those who have already written business plans and presented their companies to venture capitalists. The truth is that writing a compelling business plan and presenting yourself in person to interested investors are talents that can and must be learned and mastered. How effectively do you communicate? How convincingly do you sell yourself and your company? These are among the questions every last one of us must face.

The Grabber

Whether in the Executive Summary, which is the first section of any business plan, in the opening moments of a formal conference pitch, or even in a chance encounter (they do happen), the first impression you make is crucial. Right then, at the beginning, you *are* your company. The clarity of your goals, the sharpness of your reasoning, the conviction you bring to bear—all these make an impression, and so, in person, do your appearance, the sound of your voice, the articulateness of your speech, your confidence, your poise. A mediocre or middling first impression can be overcome, but it leaves you and your enterprise immediately at a disadvantage. Make a great first impression and the audience is yours.

Many people, particularly in conference presentations like a Springboard forum, look for a hook or gimmick to capture their audience's attention—the stacks of magazines Kim Fisher toted onstage at the Oracle Center, for example—but the same principle applies to any form of presentation. If you don't convey in the opening moments of your pitch, or the opening paragraphs of your written proposal, what is special about your company, its products, its services, and how you're going to make money on them—well, you may not get to do it at all. The target investor may already have tossed your plan.

We live in a sound-bite culture. We must get our messages out fast, loud, and clear, in concise, precise English, or the people we most want to attract will have tuned us out. This is particularly true of professional investors. They've developed short attention spans in self-defense. As a group, they are constantly bombarded by pitches and business plans from entrepreneurs. One midsize venture-capital partnership I know estimates that it receives 5,000 business plans a year. It may invest in five to ten of these companies. That's at best one in five hundred.

Experienced investors, like experienced editors in publishing companies, have trained themselves to determine in the first paragraphs of a submitted text whether to read on. Most of the time, they won't. Sometimes this may be simply because the business in question doesn't fit their area of interest, but much of the time it is because the presentation itself is uncompelling and unconvincing.

If this sounds unfair—if you want to shout, "Wait a minute! Let me finish, please! I'm just coming to the good part!"—you should remember that VCs are reflecting the business world in general. Presentation—presentation of yourself, presentation of your enterprise—is a skill you must have, whether it comes to you naturally or whether you learn it through practice and from mentors.

The good news is that these things can be learned. Attention to detail is an acquired skill. The so-called elevator pitch can be mastered as well as the conference pitch, and you don't have to be Hemingway to learn to write a compelling business plan in clear, jargon-free English. These skills have become essential to any modern business enterprise.

Sizing Your Market

One thing all VCs look for is your awareness of your own market.

How big is the market for what you're doing? How many competitors are there now? How many new competitors might be out there in one, three, five years? Won't your very success entice bigger companies into doing exactly what you're doing? What will you do if that happens? Alternatively, what can you do to prevent it?

When I hear a Springboard presenter say her company has no competition—and we've had it happen despite our best efforts—I wince. I know investors are already dismissing her. "There is *al-*

ways competition," says Susan Segal of JP Morgan Partners, a New York Boot Camp panelist and as sophisticated a venture capitalist as there is. "The questions are, How are you different? And how will that bring you market share?"

You, the presenter, must assume the people you are pitching know your market at least as well as you do and will catch any attempt to gloss over its realities. This is because, with rare exceptions, VCs tend to limit their investments to markets in which they've trafficked before. Therefore, investors who are going to be interested in your enterprise will already have built up a level of market sophistication and expertise that may well match or even outstrip your own.

One thing a smart investor is likely to look for—either in your business plan or your oral pitch—is how well you know your major customers. If he or she doesn't find this out immediately, it's sure to come up again if you're lucky enough to get to the due-diligence stage when your prospective investor may well want to interview some of your customers. Even before then, you will be judged not only on the alliances and relationships you have already cultivated but also on those you have failed to make. For instance, as I mentioned in the case of Jill Card's IBEX and Susan DeFife's StreamingText, many fledgling high-tech enterprises are business-to-business based, and those with innovative technologies may require alpha and beta testing periods to make sure they work. Be prepared for the question "Who has already agreed to try your product?"

In general, the stronger your affiliations—with customers and with strategic partners—the more impressed venture capitalists will be. Networking is critical to their business; they expect it to be to yours.

The A Team

A key element in your business plan, as in your oral presentation, will be your management team. Experienced investors know that great founders do not necessarily succeed in leading their companies past the innovative stage and managing their growth and profitability. As Paul Pollock, a New York attorney, put it to the new presenters at one Springboard Boot Camp, "For every Bill Gates, there is a Steve Jobs."

Founders typically have the original idea and vision, and many are very good at inspiring others to share their vision. They are also characteristically driven by a sense of urgency to succeed. But it takes different sets of skills to lead and manage an enterprise once it has crossed the start-up threshold and reaches a certain size. Founders are often too inflexible, too demanding, too lacking in the people skills to manage a growing business. They have trouble delegating, trouble sharing power. In fact, the two sets of skills—of founder and corporate leader—are seldom combined in equal measure in the same person.

For this reason, investors will always want to know in detail about the backgrounds and experience of the leading members of the management team. They will be looking for start-up expertise (someone on the team who has been through the launch process before), domain expertise (experience in the particular field of business), and technological expertise. This last responsibility—which falls to the chief technology officer (or chief science officer in the case of biotech companies)—is of particular concern. Investors must have confidence in the CTO's know-how and reality-based experience in controlling costs and establishing and maintaining a technology budget.

An entrepreneur infused with vision and the talent to com-municate but who approaches investors without a financial offi-cer, a sales director, or a technology chief is unlikely to obtain funding on any scale. The entrepreneur may have many of these skills herself, but from an investor's point of view, the ability to attract good people, motivate them, and mold them into a cohe-sive team is a key element in the growth and success of a company.

There is, however, a fine line when investors consider manage-ment teams, and different venture capitalists, I have discovered, look for different things. Pat Cloherty, for instance, the wonder-fully sage and experienced woman who was truly an anomaly when she joined the Patricof venture-capital firm in 1970, always looks early at who owns the stock. If it's 95 percent held by the entrepreneur, Pat becomes suspicious. What's going to motivate the other members of the team? How good can they be? Where's the balance?

On the other hand, no matter how impressive the team's cre-dentials, most venture capitalists will be looking to you—the en-trepreneur—as the leader and will be weighing your leadership qualities. You are the star. If you fade into the background or de-fer overly to others, you are likely to set off questions in the in-vestor's mind: Who's really in charge here? Where's the energy coming from, the driving force that's going to break this business out?

Paul Pollock raised a tough version of this very question at our New York Boot Camp: "Would you step aside if a venture capital-ist made it a condition of funding?"

He posed the question rhetorically, but a hush fell over the room.

It has been known to happen.

How Will You Make Money?

The jargon version of this question might be, What's your business model? The "business model" is simply the assurance that, assuming all goes according to your forecasts, the company will end up profitable after x years of doing business. This is not always as easy to explain—to yourself as well as to others—as it may sound. Susan DeFife, after six years of fighting to make womenCONNECT work, concluded that the company had been based on a faulty business model. Hordes of dot-coms that failed appear now to have had no business model at all.

The hardest part of presenting a business for any entrepreneur is undoubtedly forecasting its financial future—one, three, and five years away. The farther out in time you try to plan, of course, the more pie-in-the-sky the forecasting exercise will appear. Nevertheless, it is possible to lay out a future course based on the realities of today and certain reasonable assumptions about tomorrow and to plot a month-by-month tracking system for measuring the business forecast against actual results.

As our Boot Camp panels of experts stressed, there are lessons to be learned in this regard. Your projected numbers on both sides of the ledger—costs and revenues—must be realistic and supportable, reflecting accurate assessments of the size of your market and the share of it you expect to get. These should go hand in hand with your milestones, the significant events that have already occurred in the company's early history and the timetable forward, including your exit strategy.

Cash flow is critical to any young business, and the lack of cash has wrecked many a start-up. Among other things, this means you should seek more funding from investors than you think you need. You may not get it all, or you may not get it all from a single source, but the last thing venture capitalists want is for you to show up, hat in hand, before your next planned round of financing comes due. At the same time, and they know this from having encountered it many times before, nine out of ten start-up businesses generate revenues more slowly than predicted.

The Payoff

I'm jumping to the last spot on the road map because exit strategy is an essential part of your presentation. Historically, and particularly in the go-go years of the late 1990s, venture capitalists wanted to cash in within three to five years of their investment, either through an IPO (initial public offering) or a buyout. Since the Nasdaq implosion of March 2000, IPOs in the high-tech arena have dwindled, and many companies that planned them with underwriters have been obliged to postpone them indefinitely. They will come back into vogue one day—no question—but for an interim period of indeterminate duration, venture capitalists are focusing more on the buyout potential of the enterprises they decide to support. Furthermore, recognizing that times have changed, they are tending to stretch their period of investment to seven years and even beyond in some cases. Still, VCs are not long-haul investors, and the presentation to them of a new enterprise must discuss the likelihood of potential interested buyers.

"Exit strategy" is a complicated subject for many entrepreneurs, and it is often trotted out by venture capitalists as an "explanation" for the scarcity of women-owned enterprises in the high-risk fields. Whereas men, according to the stereotypes, are restless adventurers, ready to leave their enterprises for foreign shores, women are nest builders. In practice, we found both kinds among our Springboard finalists: the "nurturers" who, having poured heart and soul into the founding of their companies, dreaded the idea of giving them up; and the "gunslingers," who were eager to reap the financial benefits of what they had created and move on. Jill Card and Jane Homan represent the former. Susan DeFife is obviously the latter. Whether or not the original entrepreneur remains at the helm after the "liquidity event," that event must be the goal, and any presentation to venture capitalists must address how it is to be achieved.

As is pointed out many times at our Boot Camps by Springboard alumnae as well as professional panelists, it is better to own, say, 10 percent of a $100 million company than 100 percent of a $1 million company, and a whole lot better than owning a zero-dollar company that has to close its doors for lack of capital. But for those who can't accept the psychological loss of control in the first case, or the possibility in a buyout situation of being deposed as CEO, then the high-risk, big-bucks way of venture capitalism is the wrong path to follow.

※   ※   ※

BECAUSE SPRINGBOARD IS GEARED TO CONFERENCE PITCHES, we place heavy emphasis on "stagecraft," and we've had a not-so-secret weapon who has contributed greatly to our success. Her name is Kim Marinucci. Everyone who has ever attended a Springboard forum has singled out the high professional flair of our presenters, and Kim, more than any other person, is responsible for it.

She is an attractive, angular, and animated West Coast blonde who has her own Palo Alto–based coaching organization called Winning Pitch. She has been a Springboard fixture since the first Silicon Valley forum, and she has become a triple threat at our Boot Camps. She gives a "Coach the Coaches" lecture, in which all the professionals who are gathered get a refresher on how they can help their protégés improve their presentations. She and a colleague then do a ninety-minute presentation-cum-seminar for the entrepreneurs called "Mastering the VC Conference Pitch." In addition, she reviews and critiques the entrepreneurs' "elevator pitches."

Kim asks the key questions:

What feeling do you convey? (Warm and fuzzy? Chilly? Enthusiastic? Confident? Scared out of your wits?)

How do you look?

How do you sound?

She has the coach's critical eye, and that rare ability to pick up the tics and tendencies of presenters-in-training while simultaneously giving them confidence. It is Kim who coaxes Springboard's entrepreneurs out from hiding behind the podium and teaches them how to "occupy" the space of their stage. And she convinces even the shyest among them to say finally, "Hey, we can do that too."

She does it, in part, by breaking down the elements that contribute to making a good impression:

Your gestures

"Bigger is better," Kim says, "but so is fewer." The gestures you do make should be descriptive of what you're saying. Your hands should depict the word-picture of your voice. You should avoid small, hesitant hand movements that only make you seem nervous.

Eye contact

Kim's suggestion is to focus on one person at a time, one sentence at a time. This is the best way, she says, to get rid of those awkward "ums" and "ahs" that convey hesitation and uncertainty, also the best way to keep from speaking too quickly. Even as you speak to an audience, it's as though you are having a series of brief one-on-one conversations.

Your movements

The key is to "stroll purposefully" while onstage, that is, to walk while you're pausing in your pitch. This will keep the audience's attention and permit you to collect your thoughts. Kim's rule of thumb is to take three steps, then stop and continue talking.

The way you sound

You don't have to be a professional public speaker to learn how to project your voice and modulate it between high and low registers, loud and quiet timbres, fast and slow rhythms. The goal in any conference pitch—but it will also stand you in good stead in any presentation you're called upon to make—is to convey the impression of confidence and enthusiasm on the one hand (which comes in part from your mastery of the materials of your presentation) but also a relaxed and conversational easiness. You want to be liked, to be sure. But more important, you want to be believed.

People have often asked me how I gained my own skills as a presenter and how I became comfortable addressing the media and large audiences. In fact, I started at an early age. In the ninth grade, I had to figure out how to get up at the microphone in front of an assembly of 1,200 students, grades nine through twelve, and command their attention. Through trial and error, I learned my own version of many of the things Kim teaches—the important gestures, the focus on an audience of one, and, in a more general way, how to project a commanding presence from my five-foot-three-inch frame and youthful voice. I did it all out of a strong sense of self-preservation—my audience, remember, was an unruly pack of my peers—but once I'd mastered the skills, I came to love the power of the microphone and the presence at center stage. Later, in my professional career, I was able to add to my repertoire, learning, for instance, the power of "breaking the plane" by moving away from the stage and into the audience, a technique television talk-show hosts use to great effect.

As I've already mentioned, one of the great no-nos of presenting is memorizing. Kim Marinucci and the other Springboard coaches permit entrepreneurs to work from notes, and the PowerPoint slides that typically accompany their presentations are as much reminders to the speakers as they are highlights for the benefit of the audience. But the memorized pitch, either in a conference or in a one-on-one presentation, inevitably falls as flat as a pancake. The presenter is no longer a thinking human being; she is too busy remembering. And heaven help her if she is distracted from the single track of her memory, which can lead straight to stage fright and freezing up, or if—as happens—someone interrupts her with a question.

Some women entrepreneurs, we've found, have a natural stage presence that needs only to be refined in our coaching process, but many don't. Even those who don't, though, can improve their performance through practice—practice in front of a mirror, practice by talking to others, practice by reading aloud to children, practice even by storytelling. In fact, a key element in Kim Marinucci's coaching has always been the idea of storytelling. The presentation of a business can be turned into a compelling story—*your* story—rather than a dry recitation of facts and numbers. You don't have to be a stage actress to illustrate your pitch with anecdote, example, humor, and metaphor and to do so with polish and, above all, concrete, jargon-free language.

Personalizing Your Pitch

At Springboard we push the presenters to inject the personal, to find a particular way of describing or dramatizing the business of their companies, be it anecdotal or metaphorical. The presentation of companies to investors has, inevitably, a certain sameness. A business plan is a business plan, and the investment community insists on having it in a prescribed form and format. A full day of oral presentations, like a week's supply of business plans, would inspire one huge communal yawn were it not for our behind-the-scenes efforts to encourage individuality. The great danger of a system like Springboard's is overpreparation and the imposition on the presentations of what could be called a "Springboard style." In her sessions, Kim constantly stresses these points: Be yourself. Enjoy yourself.

There is another Boot Camp feature, thanks to Kim, that is unique to us as far as I know but that can be wonderfully useful to anyone for whom pitching is important. The entrepreneurs are told in advance that "it" is going to happen. Many of them complain. "I can't do that!" Or "Nobody can do that! It can't be done! What's the point?"

But of course, "it" can be done. And there's a very real point to learning how.

"It" is the elevator pitch.

During the morning session of Boot Camp, the entrepreneurs are taken one by one from the proceedings into a separate room where they are required to give a one-minute pitch for their company before a video camera. Sixty seconds, not a second more.

Sixty seconds—the duration of a chance encounter in an elevator or at a cocktail party or in the corridors of a venture-capital fair. There are moments in life when sixty seconds is all you'll have to make an impression, and you'd better be able to make good use of the opportunity.

And it *can* be done. Sixty seconds is, in fact, a relatively long time. Sixty seconds is the length of the longest commercials that run on the broadcast media, and, as we know too well, this is ample time not only to deliver a message but to repeat its selling points ad nauseum. Try counting sixty seconds and you'll see how long it feels. Try holding your breath for sixty seconds and it will seem like an eternity.

Yes, a whole company can be presented in sixty seconds. All it takes is formulating a well-conceived description and being focused and articulate. And practicing.

Try it.

The beauty of the taped elevator pitch is that you can do it yourself. You need only a one-minute timer and a loaded video camera. It is positively amazing how fast you can improve from one taping to another simply by observing yourself in action and checking out those key features—stance, movement, gesture, voice. Although Kim Marinucci can't be delivered in person to coach every reader of this book, there are professional coaches who do what she does sprinkled around the country, particularly in the major new-economy centers. Anyone for whom pitching is a fact of life would do well to look for help of this kind.

※　※　※

WHAT CAN'T BE DUPLICATED, OF COURSE—AND THE GREAT-est single contribution of Springboard, according to our alumnae—is the human capital we offer: that is, the chance to network.

Network, network, network. That, as I've already said and will repeat, is the constant message we press upon our entrepreneurs. Cast as wide a net as possible.

Boot Camp, scheduled some six weeks before the Springboard forum, is where our presenters first meet their sister entrepreneurs and where exchanges of information and encouragement begin. They also meet their coaches and the whole battery of volunteer lawyers, accountants, venture capitalists, and Springboard alums who make up the panels of experts and join in the coaching process. All these professionals, it must be remembered, are out looking for new business themselves. Many specialize in start-up businesses, which is why we want them on our panels and coaching staffs in the first place. From their point of view, the chance to meet twenty-six potential clients, be it for a handshake or an exchange of business cards—or even a fast elevator pitch—brings self-interest level with altruism.

Although the Springboard experience isn't available to every would-be entrepreneur, there are any number of women-in-business groups and organizations all over the country, certainly in every major commercial center, whose mission is to help women in start-up situations. We have been allied with many of them in our Springboard activities, and I have found them invariably smart, well-connected in their regions, and more than eager to help. Seek them out. They are a font of useful information, and, even more, they can offer entrée to others who are drawn together by a common interest—entrepreneurs, investors, and professionals alike. These are the people you must meet, must talk and listen to and do business with. There's no question but that the "human capital" side has been the secret Springboard ingredient, and it is what you must begin to develop for yourself at every opportunity.

Network, network, network!

9

Going for the Deal

IN THE LAST CHAPTER, I MADE A LEAP FROM ELEMENTS OF presentation to exit strategy, jumping over the stages in between. I'll go back now and assume you've made contact with a targeted venture capitalist, either through a conference pitch à la Springboard or through a friend of a friend of a friend who has persuaded the VC in question to read your business plan. (Remember that venture capitalists unashamedly admit that most of their investments come about through recommendations. Most VCs won't even open the envelope containing your business plan if it comes in over the transom.) You're now ready for that first crucial meeting. The twelve-minute pitch you've practiced will now become an hour-long one, face-to-face, in which your business plan will be turned inside out and you'll be questioned within an inch of your life about your company.

One bit of advice: Bring help if you need it (if, that is, you are on shaky ground on any aspect of your business).

But first let me share with you what is known about this strange financial breed—the venture capitalist—who has been so important to the fortunes of the high-risk entrepreneur.

In the first quarter of 2001, venture capitalists invested a total of $11.7 billion in 1,072 companies, or an average of $10.94 million per company, according to Venture Economics, an industry source. This compared unfavorably with the first quarter of 2000, at the height (and as it turned out, the end) of the "feeding frenzy," when $26.68 billion was invested in 1,751 companies, or an average of $15.24 million per company. The first quarter of 2001 more closely aligned with the first quarter of 1999, when $11.88 billion was invested in 874 companies, or an average of $13.59 million.

It is interesting to note the companies' stage of development in 2001 when they attracted venture capital. Expansion, or mid-stage, companies captured almost half the dollars, accounting for 48.7 percent of all capital investments. Early-stage companies captured 27.7 percent of the total, and later-stage companies got 22.6 percent, also according to Venture Economics. Buyout-stage companies reaped a mere 0.9 percent.

By region, Silicon Valley continued to land the lion's share of capital in spite of the devastation that had affected many portfolios in 2000. The northern California region placed 31.4 percent of all venture capital in the first quarter of 2001. In distant second place was New England at 13.5 percent, then New York at 11.9 percent and southern California at 9.4 percent.

But these are purely numbers. In the course of my travels, I've met a great many venture capitalists—East and West Coast and Chicago in between, young and old, life sciences–oriented and Internet aficionados—and one observation I can safely make about them is that there are few generalizations that hold for all. They are overwhelmingly white and male. Their investment philosophy is—or has been—to go for high-risk, high-return, quick-return opportunities. That is the promise they've made to their limited partners. They tend to specialize. Whereas the larger firms may have partners who mine different industries, individual VCs prefer to stick to one or two fields, developing the kind of expertise and connections that can be cultivated and expanded, with one investment leading to another. Some VCs like to come in early in a company's history; others prefer to wait until a second or third round of funding, letting the angels go first. They work almost entirely by networks—overlapping and informal buddy systems that include entrepreneurs themselves, professionals, investors, and other venture-capitalist firms, for it is not uncommon for one VC to bring in another to share in a funding. (Still, there are VCs who distinctly prefer to go it alone.) The buddy system in and of itself is hardly specific to venture capital; it permeates the entire Wall Street community, where old-school ties are still hugely important. But the system explains why women entrepreneurs were out of the loop for so long, and why, in breaking through, they must somehow be "better" than their male counterparts.

Many VCs are young—as could be expected in a new-economy-oriented field—and some of the better-known firms were formed only in the mid-1990s. But there are others, like Patricof Associates, that have been plying their trade with great success since the 1960s and where partners who have been aboard from the beginning are still doing deals with great gusto. I'm thinking of someone like Pat Cloherty, one of the great figures of venture capital in New York and someone I've admired for years, who joined Patricof in 1970 and still sits on a half dozen boards of start-ups in which she previously invested.

All venture capitalists share a mea culpa as a class for having contributed to the speculative hysteria of the late 1990s, although the culpa, when you push them, often is attributed more to someone else, such as the underwriters and mutual fund managers and mergers and acquisitions specialists who joined in the frenzy. In other words, if the underwriters hadn't been promoting new issues with wild abandon, the VCs would have been less willing to invest in any start-up with a dot-com behind its name and an enticing business plan.

Be that as it may, VCs have suffered fallout. Increasing numbers of their investments have tanked, and, as one of them ruefully put it, they have "a lot of sick patients" on their hands. Weaker VC firms have gone under. Some have merged or, like the once high-flying Flatiron Partners, have moved in with their sponsors (J. P. Morgan Chase in Flatiron's case). Furthermore, at least in the Internet world, there has been some measure of technological slowdown. Technologies have never grown on an even curve. In the twentieth century, for example, there were many revolutionary breakthrough inventions—from the automobile to the PC and the microprocessor—that spawned whole arrays of new and ancillary companies. Some of these survived to become the powerhouses we know today; others were either swallowed by the larger ones or vanished into oblivion. But a period of maturing and consolidation invariably follows the breakthrough years. Some VCs believe this has now happened across the so-called knowledge industries, with the notable exception of biotech, or life sciences. There the mapping of the human genome and the exploding field of regenerative medicine are spurring hosts of exciting new spin-off enterprises.

But just as there was a high dose of "irrational exuberance" in the bubble of the late 1990s, to quote Alan Greenspan, so now, in the early years of the new century, we've fallen into an irrational gloom. This is all the more palpable, understandably, in the New York financial community, which suffered the crippling blow of September 11, 2001. Dot-com has become dot-bomb; icons of the late 1990s like the *Silicon Alley Reporter* have closed their doors; and the direst predictions have accompanied the downswing of the economic pendulum.

Venture capital, however, has not dried up. There is still money out there for high-risk investing—a lot of it—and there are signs already of newer technologies that will be transformed into the promising commercial ventures of tomorrow. But the mood of the moment is clearly cautious. The venture capitalist's question to the entrepreneur in search of funding remains the same: "How can I use your assets to create a stream of revenue for me and my partners?" But the pressure on the entrepreneur to support her response with balance sheets and income statements has become intense compared with that period in 1998 and 1999. Then, in the words of one nostalgic cynic, anyone who had a business plan and could breathe got funding. Now, entrepreneurs are forced to take their businesses further along on other types of financing before seeking venture capital.

In the long run, this new realism, with its increased rigor, will prove to be a good thing. As *Wired* magazine recently opined, the high-tech stock-market crash of 2000 and the resulting shakeout of the dot-coms may well have been prerequisites for the true dawning of the new economy. But in the short run, an equally rigorous preparation and self-awareness on the part of the entrepreneur are prerequisites to "doing the deal."

%% %% %%

So there you are, sitting across the table from the venture capitalist. By this time he has assessed your company on paper and its potential value to his limited partners. He may well have uncovered pitfalls and problem areas that lie before you, formed his opinion of your company's strengths and weaknesses, and gauged the quality of your senior colleagues—again on paper. He likes what he sees, or he wouldn't be sitting there. He likes the idea of your intellectual property, the proprietary technology that is going to propel your business to prosperity. (Presumably you've come armed with your patent-pending documents.) You in turn have investigated him and his potential as a resource—not solely financial—to your company. He may have one or two colleagues with him. If the negotiations go beyond this first meeting, you certainly will want a seasoned professional at your side—not just a lawyer but a lawyer well versed in venture-capital deals.

But this is the moment you've been waiting for, and here, based on our Boot Camp panels, are some of the questions you should be ready for:

How much money does your company need in this round?

You've certainly come with a figure in mind. So has the venture capitalist. Probably, you'll be obliged to name yours first, and you may already have stated a range in your business plan. Whatever your figure, the business plan must support it, and most important, the sum must be sufficient to carry operations through either to positive cash flow or to the next planned round of financing. Nothing distorts the relationship between entrepreneur and venture capitalist more than for the company to run out of operating funds between investment rounds and the entrepreneur forced to go looking for more. Even in today's more tightfisted climate, most venture capitalists, whether they will admit it or not, would rather err on the upside than on the down.

You may or may not get all you need from one investor. Some VCs welcome company—a means, among other things, of sharing the risk and diversifying their portfolios with other investments. But others, having decided to bet on your company, will want it all.

How will the new infusion of funds be used?

You would think this point was axiomatic, but a surprising number of fledgling entrepreneurs can't give precise answers. You should have specific tasks and numbers at the ready, including a contingency fund in case you can't meet your forecasts (through no fault of the company). As you will hear repeatedly, revenues are always slower to come onstream than is forecast. Expenses never are.

What is the valuation of the company?

This is the key number, sometimes referred to as your prevaluation, or the value put on your company before new investments, and there may be a lot of haggling over it. In many negotiations, it is the major issue, for it leads directly to considerations of equity sharing and control. Simply put, the lower the prevaluation of the company, the larger the slice the venture capitalist can justify for himself and his investors in exchange for funding. And vice versa.

The problem is that with a young company, the classical methods of valuation don't fit. Book value, a balance-sheet measurement—that is, the excess of assets over liabilities—certainly exists, but it is really only useful in measuring value if you are planning to close the doors tomorrow (in which case you would doubtless show a negative book value). Profits—an element in the price-earnings ratio used to measure publicly held companies—probably don't exist on your income statement, and discounted cash flow, another common measurement tool, is in your projections for tomorrow, not in today's numbers. Valuation is all "on the come," then, and in your respective calculations, you and the venture capitalist are likely to come up with very different interpretations of the projected numbers. Springboard has always counseled its entrepreneurs to be rigorously realistic in their forecasts of costs, revenues, and profits, but what is realism to a true believer can be fantasy to a skeptic, particularly when the projections apply to the out years of your forecast. Even the contemporary value of tangible assets such as inventory and receivables is subject to debate: Is the inventory salable at full value? Are the receivables collectible, and when? Underlying such differences of opinion, like it or not, is the VC's natural desire to get the biggest bang for his investors' bucks and the entrepreneur's equally natural wish to keep as much of the bang as she can while getting the funding she needs.

Valuation issues are at the heart of the deal and have been deal breakers many times. At the end of the day, when the VC puts his set of numbers on the table—$X million in funding in exchange for Y percent of the shares—you, the entrepreneur, will have to wrestle with some tough questions.

How much equity are you willing to give up in exchange for funding?

You will certainly have encountered the equity-sharing issue before—with angel investors, friends and relatives, and particularly with your management team. By the time you are ready for venture capital, you will be expected to have your management team in place, ready to move the company from a purely entrepreneurial state up toward a more corporate way of running a business. Attracting a strong and experienced management team will already have obliged you to part with shares in the enterprise.

As your company grows, you will be increasingly forced to accept the idea of sharing power and profits with others. (Venture capital, as I've noted, is not a good source of funding for control freaks.) However, any smart venture capitalist—and most of them, in my experience, are very smart—will realize that you and your team must remain highly motivated. The last thing the VC wants is a disgruntled management. This fact is your ultimate leverage. Don't forget it in your rush to get funding. It should permit a fair negotiation and a balanced conclusion.

How much control are you and your management team willing to relinquish, and in what form, in exchange for funding?
Any VC will want at least one seat on your board of directors. Invariably he will want veto rights over certain types of transactions such as mergers, taking on debt, and the issuance of new stock. He will probably want the right to match any future investment offers from outside sources. He may also, in the event of a liquidation or bankruptcy, want precedence with regard to the disposing of the assets, just the way a bank would in lending money.

You, in turn, must remember that the right VC can be enormously valuable to your enterprise. Great companies, it has been said, have great investors, and if you have chosen the venture capitalist with the same care he is taking in evaluating you and your company, then you will have someone solidly linked to your enterprise and committed to its success. Chances are he is even better networked in your industry than you are and can open doors for you. He will probably know some of your customers, will certainly know some of your competitors, and may well be a source for finding good people for the management slots you still need to fill. He will also bring to your operation the kind of informed outsider judgment—a kind of tough love—

that you would or should be looking for in choosing your outside board members.

%%   %%   %%

The Term Sheet

This is the document—a short one, it is devoutly to be hoped— that will include all the salient elements of the deal once you have successfully negotiated them. It serves the same purpose as a "deal memo" or a "letter of intent" in other fields. It has no legal status until you've signed it, and there is nothing in theory to prevent you from negotiating another term sheet with a rival venture capitalist before you sign the first one. Once you sign it, however, you usually are precluded from negotiating with another investor while due diligence proceeds apace and the final agreement is being drafted by your respective attorneys. There is a lot of gray in the legal ramifications of the term sheet and in what the parties can and can't do after it is signed—the kind of gray that makes lawyers prosperous—but in principle, once a term sheet has been signed, only a major event or discovery during due diligence that cannot be reconciled should be a basis for getting out of the deal. Note, however, that in today's difficult financial climate, many VC funds have sought and found loopholes for evading financial commitments. The truth is that the deal is sealed only when the money is in the bank.

Entrepreneurs who haven't been through the process before may think of the term sheet as the deal itself and dismiss the rest as the province of the accountants and the lawyers. But a major hurdle remains to be overcome between the term sheet and the final agreement: That hurdle is called due diligence.

Due Diligence

This is the process by which the investor or acquirer of a company investigates every aspect of its activities in detail before signing a final agreement. The purpose of due diligence is to make sure (1) that everything you have said about the company in your business plan and presentations is accurate, and (2) that there's nothing you have overlooked. It entails the scrutiny of accounting files, sales transactions, corporate records, minutes of board and shareholder meetings, leases and purchase agreements and other outstanding contracts, and copies of all patents, trademarks, and copyrights. Key employees of the company will be interviewed during this period, as will suppliers and customers. Due diligence is time-consuming, tedious, and even, on occasion, disruptive, but its purpose is to prove that the valuation implicit in the term sheet is really there.

The entrepreneur seeking investors would do well to carry out her own due diligence before she even begins negotiations. Nothing is more unsettling to an interested investor than discovering skeletons in the proverbial closet that were either concealed from him or, worse, that you and your management team just didn't know about. This is why we at Springboard repeatedly encourage our entrepreneurs to identify and discuss weaknesses as well as strengths in their companies and/or problems in their business plans and to do so with candor. A careful due diligence—and venture capitalists will probably never again be as hasty and careless in this regard as they were in the go-go late 1990s—will bring them to light anyway, and nothing can kill a deal more quickly than the emergence of unhappy eleventh-hour surprises.

$$\text{\%\%} \quad \text{\%\%} \quad \text{\%\%}$$

AT OUR NEW YORK BOOT CAMP IN MARCH 2001, FAITH Charles, a lawyer and "Doing the Deal" panelist, likened the deal-making process to courtship and marriage. It's all about finding the right partner, she told her audience of fledgling entrepreneurs, and deciding how much you are ready to give up when you do. In this sense, the professionals involved on both sides become marriage brokers, and the contract that will be signed between the two parties a kind of prenuptial agreement. Unlike traditional marriage, however, this relationship is predestined to end—the "exit strategy factor"—when the investors cash out and the parties go their separate ways, but until they do, they will certainly be in bed together. And that relationship, as I have suggested, has built-in elements of tension that tend to be smoothed over when the business is going well, but that can break into destructive hostilities in difficult times. As Faith Charles noted, "Just as in marriage, the divorce can be very painful."

The most electric and in some ways radical contribution to "Doing the Deal" came from an attractive, articulate, and clearly impassioned panelist, Joan Wilbanks. An entrepreneur and Springboard alumna from Atlanta, Wilbanks had presented her company, SecureWorks, at the Mid-Atlantic Springboard the previous summer. SecureWorks, a business-to-business enterprise founded in 1999, offered the first Internet monitoring and response security service. Once its system was installed for a cus-tomer, a "securist" would constantly monitor all of the cus-tomer's Internet traffic from the company's tracking center. The moment an intruder was detected, the center would immediately respond and prevent access, and the customer would be notified without any interruption of business. In short, SecureWorks of-fered a burglar-alarm system for companies doing business over the Internet.

If ever a company looked promising and eminently fundable, it was SecureWorks. Wilbanks had carefully researched her mar-ket, noting that "58 percent of all reported computer security breaches originate from the Internet, and 41 percent of these at-tacks have generated losses in excess of $500,000. The market for Internet security services is expected to grow from $2.2 billion in 1997 to more than $7 billion in 2002."

A growing and undersupplied market, an element of propri-etary technology that had been successfully field-tested, a man-agement team that included Wilbanks with her past experience as a regional vice president of Comp USA, a chief technology of-ficer who had been director of network security for Sage Net-works, and the important and attractive feature of being a B2B-(business-to-business) based company—what could better fit the criteria of the venture capitalists? But in the downturn of 2000—her Springboard forum was held four months after the Nasdaq crash of March 2000—Wilbanks had struggled to get the financ-ing the company required. That she'd finally prevailed, in diffi-cult negotiations but to the tune of $20 million, had been at once an ordeal and an education, and she arrived before our new Boot Camp group of entrepreneurs justifiably full of her success and eager to communicate her experience.

"Work with each other," she exhorted her audience, referring to the weeks that lay ahead until the Springboard forum, "and get cracking now!" They were to organize themselves. Each of them should come up with a 100-day plan, laying out her path to funding, and they should be networking, networking, networking. As soon as they had lists of the Springboard attendees, they should be e-mailing the ones who interested them, introducing their companies, and be preparing to follow up immediately after their presentation. "Sooner rather than later," Wilbanks stressed. Springboard, she said, "gives you the creative license to be yourself and raise a lot of money. Take it." She gave the entrepreneurs a checklist of issues they must be ready to deal with, among them:

- What did you do with investors' money in round one (or the previous round)?
- What will you do with this money?
- What should you guard for yourself?
- What should you give up?

Wilbanks had some radical, tough-minded responses. "Your success," she said, "will be judged by what you are willing to let go of. The most important thing to guard for yourself is your own integrity." The entrepreneur, she stressed, had to do what was best for herself, for her shareholders—*all* her shareholders—and for her employees. "Don't let greed overcome logic," she said, "and always stand behind your word."

She gave the valuation issue top priority and recommended an interesting negotiating strategy of letting the venture capitalist himself set the valuation. The attitude of the entrepreneur to the VC should be, "We're not worried about the valuation. We're worried about cash. First and foremost, we want to build a great company." Besides, as Wilbanks pointed out wryly, when the VC comes up with a valuation number, the entrepreneur can always say no.

Wilbanks had the same advice about board seats and voting power. She was for giving them up too. They didn't matter, in her opinion. "You don't want dumb money," she said. "You want smart money," meaning that the right venture capitalist would be an asset to the enterprise. Besides, if you, the entrepreneur, didn't respect and trust those who wanted to invest in your company and help you run it, then you shouldn't be taking their money.

Even as you pitch your company, Wilbanks told our entrepreneurs, you in turn should be interviewing the venture capitalists and checking out their references. What are they bringing to the party? Do they already have clients in your field that you can tap into as customers or strategic partners? Do they have operational know-how or, say, management expertise for a company that plans to grow from ten to five hundred employees?

Then Wilbanks got down and dirty in ways that no other panelist had.

You should also, she urged, have backup plans. Although you should never shop a deal—that is, take someone's offer to another potential investor—you should also not settle for a single term sheet without having a backup verbal deal elsewhere.

Financing does go sour, she pointed out, and term sheets can vanish into thin air.

"But as women," she challenged our entrepreneurs, "our advantage is that we multitask. We must always have Plans B, C, and D."

Compared with the other panelists that day, who tended to reflect the comfortable careers of established professionals, Joan Wilbanks was a wake-up call, a reminder that things were very tough out in the real world, that nobody was giving money away, that the entrepreneur would have to fight to hold her own. She also exuded that driven quality, that bold I'm-going-to-do-this-no-matter-whatness, that seems a key element in the entrepreneurial character.

Finally, she exuded the single-minded confidence of someone who has just won. As such, she made a terrific role model for our entrepreneurs. Any woman who arrived that day with a what-am-I-doing-here anxiety came away, at the end, with a galvanizing you-can-do-it-too message. From one of her own.

10

Direct from Broadway™

Bruce Brandwen and me premiering on Broadway

"New York, NY, December 18, 2000—Broadway Television Network announced today the high definition and surround sound recording of its third Broadway musical, the Direct from Broadway presentation of the Frank Wildhorn and Leslie Bricusse musical *Jekyll and Hyde,* starring David Hasselhoff. The longest-running show in the history of the Plymouth Theatre will air on cable and satellite pay-per-view channels worldwide in Spring 2001."

The press release went on to describe the cutting-edge digital technology that would be recording twelve hit Broadway shows over the next five years. They would be distributed via wireless and cable pay-per-view systems, direct broadcast satellite, the Internet, HDTV BroadwayCinema Screen, and home video viewing.

Broadway Television Network (BTN) happened to have a woman as chairman of the board, but she didn't take her company the Springboard route. For one thing, Springboard might have rejected her application. The company name had "Broadway" in it, after all. Wasn't Broadway a place where dreamers and charlatans gambled with the capital supplied by rich old ladies with blue hair? Why would serious investors want to be involved?

Well, if anyone can explain why to you, I can. I'm chairman of Broadway Television Network, and I have an entrepreneurial story to tell.

꧁   ꧁   ꧁

I CAME OUT OF MY USA NETWORKS EXPERIENCE WANTING not only to do something for women who were taking the entrepreneurial plunge but also to jump in myself. One early spring day in 1999, I got a call from Dan DeWolf, my attorney. Dan is a business lawyer and a deal maker, who gravitated to the new Internet economy and represented a number firms in New York City's Silicon Alley. He knew I was looking.

"I've got this guy I think you should meet," he told me over the phone. "He's put together a plan for televising Broadway shows. I don't know how real it is, but you will. I think it's probably worth a lunch with us for you to find out."

If it hadn't been Dan, I might have opted out. I was more than a little skeptical about the appeal of televised Broadway shows. No matter how much money was put into the production end, what I'd seen to date always came off a little flat on the small screen.

But I went to lunch. You never know.

There were two people and Dan waiting for me when I arrived at 57/57, the elegant restaurant in the Four Seasons Hotel on 57th between Madison and Park. One of them looked vaguely familiar, a face from the distant past. He was Bruce Brandwen, a ruggedly handsome guy—in his fifties, I guessed—with salt-and-pepper hair and warm brown eyes. His wide smile was as infectious as it turned out to be frequent, almost as though he was always about to crack a joke and couldn't wait to get to the punch line. The third person was a stylishly dressed woman, Susan Lee, whose twenty years of experience on the Broadway scene belied her youthful appearance. Susan was an entrepreneur herself and a longtime marketing executive on Broadway.

Bruce Brandwen, it turned out, had produced a number of television specials for Showtime in the early 1980s and had gotten his start producing for Qube, Gus Hauser's advanced cable system. In 1982, Bruce had produced for Qube *Duke Ellington's Sophisticated Ladies,* the first musical to be televised to a pay-per-view audience. It was shown primarily to the Qube audience in Columbus, Ohio, one of the few cable systems at the time that offered pay-per-view events, and a remarkable 15 percent of the available homes had tuned in.

The pay-per-view idea, I should point out, is almost as old as cable itself. Once the cable companies had homes wired to receive television transmissions, it was easy to block certain of those transmissions unless the subscribers paid for them. This was the idea behind all the "commercial-free" premium channels like HBO. If you wanted HBO's almost-first-run movies, you had to pay an additional subscription, or the signal that the cable lines brought to your living room was blocked. From here, it was but a short step to letting subscribers buy individual programs, initially by calling the cable company and ordering their choice.

Pay-per-view and sports seemed made for each other. But although certain great sports events might have seemed perfect for it—the Super Bowl comes naturally to mind—they were so popular they could reap far bigger revenues from the television networks than from pay-per-view fees. Furthermore, there was always the fear that an audience accustomed to watching an event free on television would rise up in anger or, worse, fade away if they had to pay a ticket price in order to watch it.

Boxing, however, was a different story. Boxing was a television staple from the beginning, partly because of the relatively confined space of the ring and the limited number of participants. But, with the exception of an occasional heavyweight championship, it never appealed to a truly mass audience, and its fans were almost exclusively male. Pay-per-view was the logical answer, the more so because the target audience was accustomed to paying a king's ransom for ringside seats at the live event. Pay-per-view boxing became a bargain, and soon enough, the promoters of the sport began demanding, and getting, enormous guarantees for the PPV rights.

In time, "professional" wrestling followed, but virtually all other attempts to exploit the PPV market failed commercially or, as in the case of certain sports teams like the Los Angeles Dodgers, were limited to local territories. Pay-per-view films brought in some business, particularly from hotel rooms, but the growth of home video limited the market. In that context, what had seemed in the late 1970s and early 1980s a found-money source of revenue for both cable operators and producers, and had the Hollywood moguls rubbing their hands in anticipation, later faded into a largely forgotten niche.

Today, the biggest events on pay-per-view are the heavyweight boxing matches, which, at their peak, have drawn 2 million buyers out of 44 million pay-per-view homes. That's a little less than a 5 percent buy. Most events now offered on pay-per-view bring in less than 1 percent. The 15 percent draw of *Sophisticated Ladies* was unheard of, but the event had such minimal total exposure in 1982 that no one paid attention and there was no sequel.

For some of us, though, old dreams die hard. Bruce Brandwen had never given up the idea of bringing the Broadway musical to television, and now, in the late 1990s, new technological developments on the one hand (among them high-definition television and digital transmission) and changes in the marketplace on the other had spurred him to form a new company, Broadway Television Network. It was true, he and Susan Lee admitted, that the theater owners, producers, and investors who formed the old-guard Broadway establishment were skeptical about anything new. But the old guard itself was undergoing a generational change, and the new blood on Broadway—which included the Disney company—was open to different ways of building and exploiting its entertainment properties. Over the past four years, Bruce told me at lunch, he'd been negotiating with the fourteen—yes, fourteen—labor unions without whose support he would never be able to televise a Broadway show. He'd reached agreement with thirteen of the fourteen and was closing on the last, the all-powerful musicians union.

On another front, though—raising capital for the venture—Bruce needed help, and that was why Dan DeWolf had brought us together. The BTN business plan called for an investment round of $10–$15 million, which would allow for the filming and exploitation of two full-length musicals, but even in the free-wheeling investment climate of the late 1990s, Bruce had discovered that he needed a heavyweight on the team—someone with high credibility in the television world—to help him raise it. Enter Kay Koplovitz.

I didn't say yes on the spot, but I didn't say no either. By this time, in addition to my work on a variety of corporate boards and the National Women's Business Council, I was also involved in another venture, Wise Bear, a wellness company, and later in Working Woman Network, which had set out to marry two magazines that had undergone various vicissitudes and ownerships, *Working Woman* and *Working Mother,* with a highly ambitious Internet service. I joined the board of Working Woman Network in 1999, became CEO in 2000, and after a not altogether satisfying experience, returned the company to its magazine roots under new management in summer 2001. Broadway Television

Network, meanwhile, in some kind of weird and wonderful circling of fate, took me back to my business and media beginnings.

I went to see what Bruce had to show so far, and I was simply blown away. It was like nothing I had ever seen before. I will come back to it, but I began to make some calls. My first, I remember, was to Bill Haber, one of the founders in the 1970s of the celebrated Creative Artists Agency in Hollywood. When, some fifteen years later, the owners of CAA cashed in their chips, Bill headed back east where he devoted himself to Save the Children. He also put some of his energy and resources into producing Broadway shows, some of which were musicals.

"Gee, Kay," he said, after I'd described what we had in mind, "it sounds interesting but awfully tough. The unions for one thing. What are you going to do about the unions? It's hard enough to get them in line for a stage production."

I told him that Bruce had already made huge progress in that direction.

"I'm intrigued by the opportunity myself," I said. "What do you think? Do you want to explore it further?"

"No, thanks," Bill answered forthrightly. "I hope you make lots of money, Kay, and get the corporate jet, but it just isn't for me."

I was to hear a lot more skepticism, as well as some encouragement, but the further I pursued the idea, the more convinced I became that we were onto something. In the explosion of cable channels during the 1990s, one largely forgotten area of programming was the performing arts. Various people had tried. None had found the right formula. But that didn't mean there wasn't one, and it could well be that pay-per-view was part of the answer for this specialty audience.

On the technological side, there was the development of high-definition television (HDTV), a new technology standard that produced pictures of amazing quality, and 5.1 sound, comparable to the Dolby sound found in the best movie houses. There was also the prospect of digital projectors in movie theaters. Theater owners could expand their offerings beyond film to other digital sources, and HDTV could play a role in the development of new programs for local multiplex theaters.

At the same time, ticket prices for live entertainment had gone through the roof. In 2000 movies hit $10 in New York City. Front-row seats for Knicks games at Madison Square Garden went for $1,200—that's per seat, per game. While ticket prices for baseball, football, and other sports weren't raised that brazenly, the choice seats in many American arenas were now being sold to corporations. The so-called little guy, when he wasn't being squeezed for his second-tier seat, was having his wallet picked clean by the concession stands. On Broadway, tickets for musicals climbed steadily to $90. In 2001 market forces took over when the megahit *The Producers* appeared. Ticket prices were upped shortly after the show opened to $100—and you still couldn't get a ticket. Later in the year they were hiked again for the best fifty seats in the house—to $480—in an effort to undermine the scalpers.

Also during the 1990s, Broadway—its theater and particularly its musicals—had become big business, a "brand" in and of itself with mass and truly international appeal. An estimated 40 million tickets were sold to Broadway shows in the United States each year, but only approximately 11 million of them in New York City. The remaining theater goers saw touring and regional productions in the 100 major U.S. markets. Of the approximately $1 billion earned by Broadway shows each year, two-thirds of it came from outside New York.

Maybe it had all started with *Oklahoma*, but through the 1970s and 1980s and into the 1990s, certain musicals like *A Chorus Line* and *Cats* had become veritable institutions on Broadway. They had been succeeded by the likes of *Phantom of the Opera, Les Misérables, The Lion King, Beauty and the Beast,* and a procession of revivals, from *Chicago* and *Cabaret* to *Kiss Me Kate.* The Broadway Musical, as a brand, had reached a pinnacle of popularity and profitability that seemed to have transcended even the thumbs-up thumbs-down critics of the *New York Times.*

Meanwhile, the producers of megahits discovered gold in the rest of the world. The West End in London, of course, had long been a home to the made-in-America musical, and road shows had traveled to the wilds of the rest of the English-speaking world. Then in the 1990s, Japan became big business for the American hit shows, and so did Europe, as our pop culture seemed to take over the world.

I took all these elements into account. I added another self-evident fact: The live Broadway musical show, high-ticket and name-brand though it was, was still severely limited in capacity. (The average Broadway theater seats 1,470, so even in a sold-out year, only 611,520 customers can see that show.) I factored in digital projectors and Dolby "E" 5.1 surround sound and concluded that we had the makings of a business—a potentially great business for a targeted audience.

In April 1999, I worked out a deal with Bruce to become chairman of Broadway Television Network in exchange for equity. I wouldn't be involved in the day-to-day running of the company, but I pledged to help raise the needed capital, and I even made a modest investment of my own. With the team in place, we were ready to go raise money.

I'M PRESSING THE PAUSE BUTTON FOR A MOMENT. ONE OF the major marketing and business developments of the 1990s was the emergence of brands—of brand-name recognition—and particularly of the spinout of duplicate content in a number of different product lines. The brand name has been with us for at least as long as the advertising business, but it has become ever more important in commerce, particularly with the development of new media. People who have understood this significance, either consciously or intuitively, have reaped huge benefits.

I can think of no better example of what I'm talking about than Martha Stewart. Some twenty years ago, Martha was running her small catering business out of her house in Westport, Connecticut, when a publisher, impressed as a guest of hers, offered her a contract to do a book. That book, *Entertaining,* was published in 1982 and, thanks in part to Martha's enormous drive and skill as a promoter, became a lasting best-seller. But the book was only the start of an amazing entrepreneurial adventure. Today, the Martha Stewart empire includes a magazine, *Martha Stewart Living,* a series of television and radio programs, a website called marthastewart.com, a mail-order operation called Martha by Mail, and a retail line sold at Kmart. Much of the Martha Stewart enterprise came about because of a chance meeting (on the slopes of Mount Kilimanjaro!) between Martha and Sharon Patrick, a onetime McKinsey consultant who understood the power of a multimedia brand strategy and helped Martha extend her domain far beyond what anyone would have thought possible. Today, numerous celebrities have gone to school on Martha—in the magazine field alone there are *O* and *Rosie's,* attempts to capitalize on the immense popularity of Oprah Winfrey and Rosie O'Donnell—but no one has yet come close to matching the model.

Martha Stewart and Broadway are *brands*. They may have nothing else in common, but just as Martha's business takes content and exploits it through a number of media outlets, I saw the same potential in Broadway Television Network.

%. %. %.

I HAD EARMARKED A NUMBER OF VENTURE-CAPITAL FIRMS for Bruce and me to approach about BTN, but I thought it at least as important to go after Broadway theater owners and their backers and the cable and satellite companies. In addition to the funding they could offer, we needed to build trust in both communities: What better way than to invite them inside from the beginning?

My first call, on the owner front, was to Gerry Schoenfeld. Gerry is chairman of the Shubert Theater Organization, a crusty and pragmatic lawyer, and dean of Broadway theater, whom I'd known for many years in and around New York. We weren't fast friends, but there was mutual respect between us, and I knew he'd give me a hearing.

This he did, though at first with considerable skepticism.

"If what you're doing is as good as you say it is," he objected, "and people can see it on TV, why would they bother coming to the theater anymore?"

His was a fear ingrained in show-business people. The movie studio moguls had once been afraid of television for the same reason—wrongly, as it turned out—and I recalled hearing the same objection all those years ago when I was selling Madison Square Garden sports. Why would people come to the arena, the naysayers wanted to know, if they could watch the game in their own living rooms?

Well, because they did. Spectators wanted to participate in a social happening with thousands of other screaming fans. They wanted to see and be seen. Most important, they wanted to bask in the sweaty glow of their sports heroes, up close and personal.

It's still true—at $1,200 a ticket, mind you, with $8 hot dogs and $5 beers.

I didn't say it was rational, did I?

The same goes for Broadway.

"Nothing will ever replace the cachet of the live Broadway show," I countered. "Of being there. The rush of the pretheater crowds, the glow of the greasepaint, the exhilarating performances of the stars. It's an event, an evening out, a special and magical occasion, and nothing can replace it. If the electronic face of Broadway is going to do anything, it'll be to promote the theater and drive more people into buying your tickets."

We sparred back and forth, but I could sense Gerry pondering my arguments, and when he agreed to think about it, I knew I'd gotten my foot in the door. Maybe not all the way in, but somewhere past the toes.

The cable operators would be excellent prospects too, I thought. After all, I had spent twenty-five years building that business, and I knew the players. Surely this would be a great networking opportunity.

I culled my list and targeted those I thought would be sympathetic to the arts. Among them were Ralph and Brian Roberts, the father-son team that built Comcast into a cable powerhouse; Chuck Dolan, a lover of the opera, owner of Radio City Music Hall, Madison Square Garden and the Knicks and Rangers, Cablevision, and a host of cable networks; and Paul Allen, co-founder of Microsoft and now a player on the cable block with his acquisition of Charter Cable, sixth-largest cable company in America.

All of them were polite enough to listen.

None of them took up the challenge.

Doggedly I went on down my list, cable operators whom I thought would benefit from new entertainment product to offer their subscribers, but my story simply wasn't playing. Why? The further I pressed, the more I grudgingly came to realize that the operators didn't care much about event television. It took a special effort to market, and they had plenty of other products that they considered easier to sell. Pay-per-view, in their vision, was a backwater of the industry.

In early June, I visited a legend in the cable business, Michael Fuchs, onetime chairman and CEO of Home Box Office. Intelligent, articulate, witty, and bold, Michael is such a skilled gamesman and deal maker you almost overlook his condescension toward those who are of no use to him. No sooner did I introduce the subject of BTN than he felt compelled to tell me of his own investment—a small one, he said, in Broadway Archives. Broadway Archives was a company formed to digitalize old television plays and relicense them to cable and satellite channels. Michael thought the two companies might be too competitive. Besides, he allowed, he didn't really believe in pay-per-view.

"I never supported it at HBO," he recalled. "In fact, I fought mightily against it. I still feel the same way."

"Okay," I said, "and I understand your point of view. But it's a different world now. You don't run HBO, and I don't run USA, so where's the harm in your taking a look?"

He still declined. He just didn't want to get involved.

As it turned out, Michael had a bigger role in Broadway Archives, later renamed Broadway Digital, than he'd led me to believe. Everywhere I went, talking to people in the business and the media about Broadway Television Network, I ran into questions about Michael. "How's Michael's thing doing?" I'd be asked. Or, "Isn't he doing the same thing you are?" I often wondered if he was asked the same about "Kay's thing."

I also struck out with John Malone. John was chairman of TCI, the largest cable operation in the nation, which he finally sold to AT&T, and he is chairman of Liberty Cable, which then had an ownership position in some ninety cable networks. John is the greatest strategist and the biggest influence on the industry, bar none. He has also backed a lot of people who ultimately became enormously wealthy, Ted Turner among them, whom John saved more than once from the brink of financial ruin.

We met for breakfast at the National Cable Show in June. John was in his usual fine form, holding forth encyclopedically on the challenges the industry faced and who was doing what to whom. When I broached my subject, he immediately began to recite the failures in the performing arts—Chuck Dolan's opera showcase, Polygram, ABC Television, even Universal.

All losers.

I went through my usual routine about how things were different now.

He heard me out, but said with a wave of his hand, "Kay, I wish you luck."

And then came the punch line.

"Since I'm on Barry's board," he went on, "I don't feel I could even consider investing in your venture. But you know, if you end up making a success of it, Barry's going to be jealous as hell. What you're doing is exactly what he wants to do."

The reference, of course, was to Barry Diller. John Malone not only was on the USA Networks board, but he also held a large position in Barry's company.

I doubt John noticed the brief flash of anger in my eyes, which was just as well.

I wasn't furious about Barry Diller, who had long coveted Bravo, one of the Rainbow Networks, and had wanted to use it to bring performing arts to television. And I wasn't angry about John either.

It was the club. The club to which I did not belong. It was the implicit notion that someone else had the inside track, be it "Barry" (in John Malone's case) or "Michael" or some other member of the old boys.

"But what about Kay Koplovitz?" I wanted to rail. "Didn't I pay my dues? Didn't I fight for this industry for twenty-five years? So what about *my* plans, *my* aspirations? Why not me?"

%% %% %%

ANGER PASSES.

I'd come aboard at BTN convinced that our support was less likely to come from traditional venture capitalists, for whom the exit would be too slow in coming, than from strategic partners who would grasp what we were doing right off the bat and who, even while running extremely successful enterprises themselves, were concerned about how to handle the new technologies looming on the horizon. The late 1990s, remember, were extraordinarily volatile times in entertainment and communications. Some companies were becoming even more gigantic, like AOL and

Time Warner; others would soon be breaking themselves up, like AT&T. Telecom companies had spent fortunes laying millions of miles of fiber optics nobody wanted—yet. Wireless was about to go down the drain—for the moment. HDTV had laid an egg—so far.

But major change was coming. Everybody knew it, but nobody knew exactly what to do about it.

In that kind of climate, a company that offered a distinctive, branded, ahead-of-the-curve entertainment product—one that was adaptable to any of the new technology delivery systems, that already had a few exclusive licenses plus union deals, and that was positioned to acquire more licenses in a hurry—that company had to be appealing, if not to the cable operators then to other investors. I just had to find them.

I finally turned to Sid Lapidus and David Libowitz, who ran the Warburg Pincus media fund and who had backed a number of companies in the cable and broadcast industries. They were intrigued with our business model, and they were quick to see our point that pay-per-view was only our first window of distribution. They understood that eventually our company could evolve into a full-time cable network, which they coveted.

There was only one problem. We were looking for a minimum of $10 million, maybe as much as $15 million, and if Warburg Pincus went with us, they wanted it all for themselves.

"We've got to invest big if we invest at all," Dave Libowitz said when we sat down for serious discussion on May 25, just before the National Cable Show. "That's how Warburg does it. After all, this isn't a large investment for us. If we like what we see in your plan, we'll need to take it all."

Encouraging, but at the same time a little unsettling. If they took it all, they could end up controlling the company at a very early stage. Not at all what we wanted. Still, we had to get ourselves off the ground.

We kept the ball rolling with Warburg, but I made it my business to continue networking with people important to the Broadway community. I went back to Gerry Schoenfeld. By a great stroke of luck, he'd been to a Knicks game at the Garden just a few nights before, and he was still astonished by what he'd seen.

"The excitement was unbelievable!" he said. "I hadn't been there in fifteen years—more—and I didn't know they put on such a spectacle. The lights, the noise, even fireworks. The whole nine yards! I guess we've fallen way behind when it comes to entertaining our customers."

I reveled in these words. Now maybe we could convince Gerry that BTN was a great electronic face for Broadway—a way to attract a whole new audience and to promote the remarkable live shows put on night in, night out in New York.

I went to see Rocco Landesman too. Rocco runs the Jujamcyn Theaters, the smallest of the Broadway theater organizations yet a powerful force in the community. Rocco had taken risks on unusual shows—he has something of the gambler in him—and later on he came through with support for us. I also pitched Roy Furman, a very successful investment banker who had joined Michael Ovitz in buying Livent, the theater company started by Garth Dubinsky. The company was in disarray—Dubinsky, among other things, had been keeping two sets of books, and lawsuits were piling on lawsuits—but Roy and I hit it off, and in the end, he not only became an investor but joined our board, where he has made a consistently strong contribution.

Not every connection worked. We pitched many venture capitalists and investment firms that hectic spring and summer of 1999. I knew a lot of the people, one way or another, and those I didn't know I networked my way into. The list included Herb Allen Jr. of Allen and Co., John Waller, a banker who brokers cable systems around the country, even J. P. Morgan. All passed. I also spent a lot of time wooing Bill Baker, the dapper bow-tied president of WNET, the PBS station in New York, whom I'd known for years and with whom I had recently partnered in support of the Charlie Rose show on PBS. What I was after from Bill and his colleagues was a collaboration to carry our productions after the pay-per-view window. I thought the fit would be perfect. Indeed, WNET's newly finished high-definition studios on West 33rd Street would have been ideal for our postproduction work, and having WNET as a partner in our venture wouldn't hurt in other respects either.

But it wasn't to be. When Bill and I finally met in late June, he'd already made a licensing deal with "Michael's company," Broadway Archives. He had acquired the rights to some seventy plays made for television, mostly in the 1950s and 1960s, and was in the process of digitalizing them and thereby restoring much of what had been shot on videotape.

Michael's company? The hell with Michael's company; we had Warburg Pincus. Richard Haigh, an investment banker and investor who'd been working with Bruce Brandwen long before I came on the scene, was heavily involved in the negotiations now, and the numbers were a-crunching when, at the eleventh hour, Dan DeWolf made another of his important introductions.

Jack Rivkin was the head of Travelers Venture Fund, part of Sandy Weill's group of companies at Citicorp. Jack is known primarily as a mover and shaker in high-tech investing, having funded a number of Silicon Alley companies with innovative technology, but he was also interested in content that could drive some of the broadband technology that, he was convinced, would one day turn the Internet into streaming video—that is, television.

Our first meeting went extremely well. Jack brought along Dirk Hall, his numbers man, who has a solid grasp for what drives businesses. As Bruce and I unfolded the story of BTN's potential, they became noticeably more interested. High-definition television, they understood immediately, would translate well into all the production windows: television, the Internet, broadband, and broadcast. "The electronic face of Broadway." They got that. They got it instantly.

By mid-July, Warburg and Travelers were running neck and neck, and we were deep into term-sheet negotiations with both. Warburg had deep pockets and an appetite for growth and future funding, but wanted a position on future investment rounds that would make it tough to get higher valuations from others. The Travelers people were more flexible. They were willing to negotiate future financing terms, but we weren't certain as to their staying power for future rounds. Certainly Citigroup had the financial resources to fund forward, but would it?

In early August, Richard Haigh and Jack Rivkin happened to be in London on other business. They met to negotiate, and Richard was on the phone back to us each step of the way as they spelled out financial terms and commitment. They came away with a handshake deal.

The die was cast. We would go with Travelers.

Even then, it took three more months to seal the deal. Among other requirements, we had to nail down our agreement with the musicians union. Funding didn't come through until November 1999. Of our $10 million, $6 million came from Travelers. The rest came from the theater owners—the Shubert Organization, the Nederlander Theater Organization, Jujamcyn, and SFX (now Clear Channels Entertainment)—and a group of individual investors keenly interested in both Broadway and high-definition technology.

We came out of the gate quickly.

%%   %%   %%

THE TRUTH WAS THAT WE HAD TO. AS THE ATTENTIVE reader will recognize by now, one drawback to BTN was that we had no proprietary technology, no technological edge. As far as digital cinema was concerned, Bruce and our colleagues had worked closely with companies like Texas Instruments in developing superior display and sound, but the proprietary technology for digital cinema was owned by companies like Boeing, QuVIS, and Dolby, in addition to Texas Instruments. Nothing could prevent our eventual competitors from going the same route and producing the same spectacular results.

As Ted Turner once said, "If you're not ahead of the curve, you're behind it," and BTN, which by the end of 1999 had a lead over everyone else, now had to consolidate it every which way. We had our multiyear union deals—actors, musicians, stagehands, house staff, video engineers, among others—and we had the strategic partners among the Broadway theater owners. Bruce had also put together a fabulous production team, all experienced in their respective domains but featuring as co–creative directors Don Roy King for television and Jerry Zaks for stage.

King, an Emmy winner, had credits that spanned five television networks, and Zaks, a four-time Tony winner, had directed innumerable Broadway shows and was the 1994 recipient of the George Abbott Award for Lifetime Achievement in the Theater. We could also now negotiate and execute our pay-per-view distribution deals with the largest cable satellite systems: inDEMAND (a consortium of AT&T, Time Warner, Comcast, and Cox), DirecTV, the DishNetwork, Cablevision, several foreign distributors, and so on. During 2000 we acquired Theatre.com, a leading theater portal that we converted into BroadwayOnline.com, and we established a video-on-demand (VOD) branch called BroadwayonBroadband and made a distribution deal with On2.com, a leader in Internet streaming and VOD.

I've saved the best for last: the show itself. We shot *Smokey Joe's Café* in January 2000, using the last live performance of its long and highly successful Broadway run. Mike Kaplowitz, our sound director, had forty-nine mike tracks from the stage, covering every conceivable sound from the show's eight performers, and the camera angles were set up in such a way that we not only caught the performers as a group and in one-on-one close-ups but got the audience too. Not long afterward, I watched the entire show for the first time. I was excited, enthralled, and felt butterflies flickering their wings all through my system.

As I told Bruce, it wasn't the same as seeing the show live in a theater. Nor was it the same as watching a filmed version, at least any film I'd ever seen of a stage performance. It was a wholly new experience, brand new, as if I were eavesdropping on a Broadway show from the wings, from the audience, and from the midst of the performers.

Fabulous.

Mine was not a unique reaction.

We've now had similar responses over and over, particularly from people experienced in show business. After one of the creators of our third production, *Jekyll and Hyde,* Frank Wildhorn, saw our version for the first time, he told Bruce, in utter amazement, that although he must have sat through the show on stage some 500 times, he had just noticed things the actors did that he'd never seen before. That happened because our cameras brought him closer than he'd ever been before.

We had a winner.

ON MARCH 10, 2001, OUR TEAM TROOPED OUT TO EDGEWAter, New Jersey, with Shari Redstone, where her company, National Amusements, had installed a digital projector for the purpose of testing our product. The occasion was the premiere of BTN's *Jekyll and Hyde,* starring the remarkable David Hasselhoff. This to me would be the real test. *Smokey Joe's Café,* after all, was more of a revue and relatively easy to film, with just eight characters. *Jekyll and Hyde* was a full-fledged musical, with book and story as well as music.

We had a packed house for the viewing, including a number of New Yorkers we'd cajoled and coerced into coming—"New Jersey? You gotta be kidding!"—and expectations of a major success. Most of the audience members were new to the experience, and I could feel it in them even as the show was running, the electricity, the rapt attention, that same sense I'd personally felt that this was something new, different, and great.

And so it turned out to be. It is now clear that BTN's cinema versions of Broadway musicals will fly—when the number of digitally equipped theaters around the country reaches a critical mass. Furthermore—and this has been a key point in evaluating and planning the business—all our tests and surveys to date have shown that although the public grumbled when first-run movie theaters in New York City raised their prices to $10, there has been no resistance to a $20 ticket for an original-cast Broadway show on a high-definition digital screen. The mental comparison is made not to the movies but to the theater experience, which can cost $100 and up on Broadway and $65 for touring companies in major-market cities.

Surveys of the audiences at digital cinemas confirmed our instincts that our product travels perfectly to the big screen. Of the people who attended the show in seven cities, 58 percent filled out our survey. In a spectacular response not even we could have hoped for, 98 percent rated the show good or excellent, and 99 percent said they would attend the next one.

We had a similar experience in November 2001 when we held the European digital cinema premiere of a Broadway show at the Odeon Theater on London's Leicester Square. The show was *Putting It Together,* starring Carol Burnett, and it was greeted by rave reviews and great audience enthusiasm. The screenings led to a contract with the Odeon Theater to feature *Smokey Joe's Café* and *Jekyll and Hyde* in spring 2002. Digital Projection, another exhibitor, sought the rights to introduce our three shows in eight theaters in Japan. UCI, yet another UK-based firm, signed all three shows for exhibition in its theaters in Manchester, Düsseldorf, Vienna, and Barcelona.

The future will be ours—once we get there. Meanwhile, I've had my own version of the white-water journey I've been talking about throughout these pages. I've also had my eyes opened to what I can only call the new reality of business in the twenty-first century. Despite the fact that I had all the strategic contacts in the industry to which BTN belonged—I was networked to the max —it was just as difficult for me to get people to write the check as it is for the most fledgling entrepreneur.

The moral, of course, is that if you believe in what you're doing, you must persist. There, I've mentioned it again, that single-minded drive we entrepreneurs all share and that women entrepreneurs, those who are going to make it, seem to possess in abundance.

Sticking to your goal and networking to the max—those are the keys. Remember, above all, it is the human capital that counts, meeting those people who already have a seat at the table and getting them to welcome you in. If you can do that, the money will follow.

11

Closing the Circle,

or

the End of

Capital Starvation

Patty Abramson

YOU MUST HAVE NOTICED IT BY NOW. PROBABLY YOU'VE been irritated by it. The entrepreneurs described in this book are all *shes*, but every time I've referred to venture capitalists, I've used the masculine pronoun.

Sorry, but there's a reason for this gender profiling. It's unfair to say that *all* venture capitalists are male—they aren't—but it's been such a male-dominated field that even the women who work in the VC firms tend to occupy "staff" rather than "line" positions. There are exceptions, to be sure, and I've named some of them—Pat Cloherty, Ann Winblad, and Susan Segal spring quickly to mind—but women who invest, and women who lead other women to invest, particularly in the high-risk sectors of the financial scene, are few and far between.

Historically this is not so surprising. Just as there were almost no women in the upper echelons of business or the professions in the middle of the twentieth century, so there were relatively few women of independent means. Those who did have independent income usually entrusted their wealth to men, if not their husbands, to manage for them. Money simply was not women's work. Remember that the rank and file of American women—our mothers and grandmothers—were given "allowances" by their husbands to take care of household expenses. They were on the dole.

To this day, many American women know next to nothing about managing money. They prefer to leave such things to their husbands. At the same time, along with other cultural and eco-nomic changes that have brought societal shifts over the past half century, women who have their own money and women who've *made* their own money are no longer a rarity.

Why are wealthy women reluctant to jump into the white wa-ter from their side of the circle and become full-fledged members of the investment class? As I researched the question, I again ran into the same self-fulfilling stereotypes:

- Women are more conservative than men.
- Women don't like risk, or the idea that they might be jeopardizing their security.
- Women aren't as good at math and sciences. They're not capable of the detailed analyses and projections that high-risk investing requires.

I'm not suggesting that it's time for American women to start stealing their kids' education savings to invest in start-up compa-nies. But in these fast-changing times, there is no part of eco-nomic life from which women, a priori, should be excluded or exclude themselves. Therefore, in this particular area of high-risk investing that interests me, I set out to close the circle.

The inspiration came to me on the spur of the moment, even as I was addressing the assembled Springboard shareholders at the Silicon Valley organizing committee meeting of April 1999. There we were, I realized, trying to bridge the divide between women entrepreneurs and venture capitalists, but those on the other side of the circle were all males. Did that have to be?

"I believe," I said, "that women could become the catalyst of early seed investing in women-led companies by becoming angel investors themselves. There are certainly enough women with a high net worth and possibly the appetite to make these high-risk investments. Why not? Why not organize women to be the supply side of the equation as well, providing the needed early capital?"

I suspected that angel investing would take some organizing. Most women, it was true, knew little about judging risk in start-up companies. I had gone through a trial-and-error period on my own, making investments and learning from my successes and mistakes. It had been an expensive self-education, one few would undertake on their own.

"But together?" I asked. "Why couldn't we learn—and profit— together?" I suspected there were enough women like me who had built up a capital reserve and would invest if they had someone to take them up the learning curve. Angel investment clubs of high-net-worth women just might be part of the solution.

I speculated to the assembled shareholders that there would be a follow-on to the Springboard agenda, one in which we could put women's capital to work. The idea sparked some heated debates later on. Longtime venture capitalist Don Lucas sent me a message via Heidi Roizen to get off that kick. Springboard, Don allowed, was a great idea, but angel investing by women would never work.

Others, though, found the argument compelling. The idea surfaced on several more occasions during the initial Springboard sessions and later at meetings convened by the Kauffman Center for Entrepreneurship and at the National Women's Business Council as well.

Among those who took up the call was Patty Abramson, who initiated an investment club in Washington, D.C., called Women-

Angels. Patty herself was a venture capitalist. Together with Wendee Kanarek and Rob Stein, she had started the Women's Capital Growth Fund in 1997, raising $30 million that they had placed in sixteen young companies, all owned by women.

Many other funds devoted to women-owned or -managed companies have sprung up like mushrooms in other parts of the country. Among these are Veridian Capital, founded by Willa Seldon and Christine Cordero; Capital Across America, started by Whitney Johns Martin; and the Cincinnati-based Isabella Fund, founded by Peg Wyant.

Patty Abramson's WomenAngels is broadly akin to Hans Severiens's Band of Angels but with several significant differences. Each Woman Angel must contribute $75,000 to the fund, no less and no more, and each has one vote. In the Severiens group, individual investors could decline to invest in any proposed enterprise, whereas members of WomenAngels are committed to participate in whatever the investment committee decides. The members are all from the Washington area, and their investments are made largely in mid-Atlantic enterprises, which may or may not be women-owned; there are no restrictions in this regard. Member-investors are encouraged to learn, encouraged to participate. They share in the tasks of due diligence; they often sit on the boards of the companies they invest in.

To date, WomenAngels has raised $6 million from 80 investors. They have taken positions in six different enterprises. These angel, or seed, investments represent a very early stage of venture capital, long before the companies in question have proven themselves. Therefore, they are higher in risk and longer in return than even the most intrepid venture capitalists would accept in their models. It is too early for Patty to predict the eventual return on investment, but she reports that although one of the companies is going to fold, most have already raised their next round of funding—the first concrete indication of success in the making.

In retrospect, women's angel funds were an idea waiting to happen. When I started mine, I organized it somewhat differently, but my motive was the same—to get women to overcome their historical timidity as investors, to educate them in the ways of start-ups and entrepreneurs, and to make money—for them and for myself. What's more, I encountered a general eagerness to participate: I discovered many women who've done well financially but who are chafing at the centuries-old limitations society has placed on women when it comes to money. It wasn't all that long ago, after all, that all credit cards were in the names of the husbands and that women, particularly when they got divorced, had practically no chance of establishing credit on their own. This, in fact, is still a major problem—the irrational, yet equally stubborn reluctance of credit organizations to accept women as credit risks even though women have proved overall a better credit risk than men. In any case, I found some women who are hungry to be educated in the high-risk, high-reward fields.

My particular fund is called Angels4Equity (A4E) and is limited to women investors. I started it with women I knew, and together we set out to recruit others who were experienced in business and the professions and who had the wherewithal to step up as investors. Our goal was to raise $6–$10 million, not a huge sum, with a minimum participation of $100,000 and an open-ended maximum, although our preference was for a $300,000 maximum. Along the way, we hired as fund manager an extremely bright young woman, Amy Wildstein, who had earned her spurs doing similar work with start-ups at Morgan Stanley and before that, Blackstone Partners. Amy is under no restrictions with regard to the investment opportunities she pursues—they can be male- or female-owned, for example—and in today's sluggish economic climate, the opportunities are numerous. No sooner did A4E announce its existence than Amy was deluged with business plans. But she is a quick study. From the flood of plans, and with the approval of our investment committee and subsequent due diligence, she quickly found our first two investments:

The AgraQuest Company of Davis, California, founded by CEO Pam Marrone, makes natural pesticides—"biopesticides"—for the organic-food-producing market. Angels4Equity's commitment was $165,000. We were fortunate to get into the AgraQuest F round of funding, because at the time the company went looking for this round, it had nearly attained profitability. As soon as the general financial climate improves, as it will, AgraQuest will be a prime candidate for an initial public offering.

Precision Therapeutics of Pittsburgh, Pennsylvania, was our other investment, to the tune of $300,000. The company was in its B, or second, round of funding. It is a biotech company, engaged in cancer research and already testing patented tissue culture assays that assist oncologists in determining the effectiveness of available cancer therapies for individual patients. It was founded in 1995 by Dr. Paul Kornblith, a renowned neuro-oncologist who has spent thirty-five years in the fields of human tissue culture, chemotherapy, and immunotherapy. We believe Precision Therapeutics will be a prime buyout candidate for a strategic partner.

I can feel in my bones that Angels4Equity is going to do well. So does Amy Wildstein, and so do our investors. But more exciting to me is the edge-of-the-seat atmosphere at our quarterly dinner meetings. It is a great plus to have among us women from very different backgrounds. Some are from financial institutions, yes, but there are also lawyers, recruiters, media professionals, doctors, and retail executives. The broad experience of the members lends richness to our discussions. Certainly my horizon has been expanded by the collective knowledge of these women, almost 75 percent of whom are new to me personally. And thus does my network grow.

Generally, we start our meetings with a short cocktail reception while people arrive. Then Amy begins by updating us on the companies already in our investment portfolio. She is followed by two prospective newcomers who present their enterprises, after which club members dig in with Q&A. The presenters are peppered with both practical and technical questions, and these come fast and furious from all around the room. The entrepreneurs are asked to stay around and mingle with us over dessert before the floor is opened to investors to express their reactions and levels of interest. This closes the evening.

Investments are not, however, subject to general vote. They are proposed by Amy to the governing board for approval, which consists at present of Penny Zuckerwise, an experienced asset manager, and me. We are assisted by able securities lawyer Rachel Arfa. We also have an advisory committee consisting of eight members who are experienced venture capitalists and asset managers, and they are asked to vet the investment as well. Before finalizing an investment, we often review the deal with other VC fund managers who have expertise in the field at hand. When possible, our strategy is to invest side by side with VC funds that have forward-funding capabilities.

We sometimes have speakers who aren't themselves entrepreneurs but offer some level of experience in investment strategies. This was the case at our second quarterly meeting, during which Melissa Krinzman, CEO of Venture Architects, spoke on her firm's qualifying benchmarks for early-stage investments. It was a succinct, step-by-step process that many in the room found enlightening.

My A4E partners—relatively sophisticated women, experienced in business and the professions—are being exposed to a new kind of activity, and they are responding with energy and enthusiasm. There is an electricity in the air at our meetings that is clearly caused by something beyond the specifics of the investments, actual or potential. I believe the dynamic factor is that the women partners of A4E and other angel investment clubs are participating, whether they are conscious of it or not, in a marked cultural change.

WOMEN ARE BOMBARDED DAILY BY "EXPERT" VOICES PROpounding this or that theory of what they should be doing with themselves and their lives. They're encouraged to stay home, raise children; alternatively, they're pushed to join the workforce. They're warned to commit themselves 24/7 to their jobs or else to demand flex-time. Now here's my voice, encouraging them to entrepreneurship, either on the entrepreneurial or the investment arc of the circle. In any case, the attraction of entrepreneurship has already taken root among women, and I can't imagine it diminishing, now or tomorrow. In the process, the business landscape of America is being transformed.

There is more to do, much more. The slice of a woman's entrepreneurial life exemplified by our Springboard initiative is just that—a slice. I chose to use it as a vehicle to illustrate what can and should be done, to prove that the power of an idea can galvanize people to cause significant change. That's one basic principle I hold to be self-evident.

In my view, we're only at the beginning of economic freedom for women. Sometimes I have to remind myself that when my grandmother set foot in this country in the first decade of the twentieth century, women were not yet permitted to own property or to vote. It's not that we haven't come a long way; it's just that if you're living it, change is not coming fast enough, and certainly not where equity and capital are concerned.

We must make more dynamic changes to access the debt markets and the more traditional bank lending. A study the National Women's Business Council cosponsored with the Milken Institute in 2000 found that although women owned nearly 40 percent of the businesses in the country and these produced nearly one-third of the GNP, they accessed only 12 percent of their debt financing though traditional banks. The five recommendations that came out of the Milken research make good sense. Among them is to change Regulation B in the Equal Credit Opportunity Act to include race and gender so that progress can be tracked. Another is the securitization of loans to women-led businesses, reducing risk to lending banks because of the opportunity to lay off risks to other financial institutions. The other recommendations involve creating new credit-sourcing models, implementing a National Capital Access Program, and institutionalizing the Economic Census reports so that we can better benchmark the progress women are making.

In the same way that we have opened the door for women entrepreneurs in the equity markets, we can open the doors to the debt markets and more sophisticated financing vehicles. It is essential to bring women owners out of the depths of capital starvation.

As has been the case with Springboard, it's important to remember that the most important capital we can create is human capital. Women simply must learn how to access the resources they need, and access means people. We've not only schooled entrepreneurs. We've taught venture capitalists, lawyers, accountants, consultants, and so on, to trust women by investing themselves—their time and effort as well as money—in women's successes. We need to do this all around the financial circle in order to create long-lasting wealth for everyone.

I believe we women can accomplish all we set out to do; we just must build our networks as we go.

12

Playing to Win

IN SPRING 2001, I WAS INVITED TO A DINNER IN WASHINGton, the intent of which was to connect women of some prominence in an informal setting. Among those attending were Lisa Benenson, then editor-in-chief of *Working Woman* and *Working Mother;* Madeleine Albright, secretary of state in the Clinton administration; Senators Barbara Mikulski of Maryland and Olympia Snowe of Maine; Iris Burnett, a founding partner of the microlending fund Count Me In; and a handful of special guests. I assumed the political issues of the day would be the topics of discussion, perhaps with a tilt toward women's concerns. But I couldn't have been more wrong.

The two senators wanted to talk about Springboard. They were very curious about the ideas behind it, how we had made it happen, how we had found the people. They also wanted to know if there wasn't some way of linking women-owned start-ups to enterprise zones, the business enclaves in certain states and areas where the federal government gives tax abatements and other benefits to participating companies and political localities.

They also wanted to know about my motivation in founding USA Networks. How did I know I could do that way back when? What obstacles had I faced, and why did I succeed?

As for Madeleine Albright, she wasn't interested in talking about the new Bush administration or her successor, Colin Powell, or the Israeli-Palestinian negotiations that had degenerated from Camp David into Intifada 2. Not at all. The topic on her mind was her own new business. In the time-honored tradition of other former cabinet officials, she was setting up the Albright Group, a consultancy in global strategies, and she was eager to hear everything I could tell her about start-ups. (No, I didn't recommend that she apply to Springboard.)

Consultants are akin to people in personal services. They don't need much in the way of funding; they need clients. What Madeleine wanted to talk about was the networking that had occurred, how I had managed in such a short time to create a national movement, and how she might learn from what we had done. She was obviously learning already, because there she was, networking with me on her own. I was impressed with the penetrating questions she asked, one of which was about the emotional problems of setting up your own business.

Beyond the basic steps—obtaining office space, hanging out the shingle, attracting talent to join you, publicizing and marketing your new services—how do you deal with the fear of failure?

"Do we all have it?" she wanted to know.

Ah, yes, I thought. Fear of failure is a common nemesis, and some of us are overwhelmed by it. Who would think, though, that this accomplished woman, an icon of American statesmanship—the woman who had stared down Slobodan Milosevic and Yasir Arafat and Kim Jung II—would have any fear at all?

"It's always there," I replied. "We all have it, but it's just a part of the entrepreneurial game. You've got to decide if the potential for success is worth dealing with the fear. There's no safety net."

She nodded in understanding. Like others doing what she was about to do, she had to learn to stare down the same self-doubts.

Reflecting on the conversation later, I thought about a message I often delivered in my speeches to women during the 1980s when I was called upon to motivate others by telling of my success in the cable industry.

The message took a different tone then. I often admonished women for lacking the will to succeed. Everyone was talking about fear of failure then too, but it seemed to me at the time that women were predetermining their fates by accepting secondary roles in corporations. They were settling for staff positions in human resources, marketing, or communications, which, important as they were, were still not line positions, the ones that generated revenues, the ones that determined success.

"Don't be afraid to succeed," I would tell them. "Fight back these fears of failure and ask yourself, 'Am I afraid to succeed? What's next if I do succeed? Will I be in line as the next CEO? Do I want that role?' If that's what you want, then *go* for it!"

Those days were different, of course. In the 1980s the game we all played was being successful in the corporate world and climbing the corporate ladder, even though, for most of us, that meant getting shoved aside on the road to the top. But over the ensuing decade, that very shoving-aside treatment led many women to take the entrepreneurial route. These women have their fears too—as one of them told me, "What's really involved is trading one set of anxieties for another"—but they are not afraid to succeed, and that's progress. Progress at last!

As for Springboard, its growing success has brought growing pains with it, and it became clear to Amy Millman and me that we would need to emerge from the shadow of the National Women's Business Council. The funding for Springboard, remember, came not from the government but from the private sector—all the corporate and professional sponsors we were able to attract. From there, it was just a short step to separate the organization from its formal government ties and create an independent nonprofit. We dubbed it Springboard Enterprises. It was born in spring 2001 with Amy Millman as president and two regional Springboard organizers, Denise Brosseau from California and Andrea Silbert from Massachusetts, as board members. After leaving my post as chair of the National Women's Business Council in June 2001, I too joined the Springboard board, as did Trish Costello from the Kauffman Fellowship Fund.

Springboard was now free to change. Still, it had accomplished a great deal in its nearly two years of existence. In its first twenty-two months, 199 companies gave presentations to the venture-capital communities of Silicon Valley, Boston, northern Virginia, New York, and Chicago. As of November 2001, they had raised over $615 million in VC financing.

Beyond raising capital in dollars, we also created human capital that we believe will prove our most lasting legacy to the companies we've nurtured. Over 2,000 members of the venture community, which includes venture capitalists, lawyers, accountants, and educators, have joined in making Springboard a success. Thanks to their efforts, a whole new generation of entrepreneurs has blossomed.

In November 2001 we presented our second Springboard at Harvard Business School, and the seventh in the series. Twenty-three entrepreneurs took the stage in front of the strongest gathering of venture capitalists yet. Even in the aftermath of the September 11 tragedies, the human-capital circle was hard at work. Enthusiasm ran high, and my faith and confidence in the entrepreneurial spirit of our country, even at a difficult historical moment, were roundly renewed.

It would be quite a success story even if it ended there.

But it doesn't.

There are people, we know, who believe Springboard should "wither away." They argue, on the one hand, that a women-only approach is exclusionary and undemocratic and, on the other, that women in business no longer need a helping hand. In an ideal world, they would be right. In an ideal world, Springboard wouldn't have been necessary in the first place. Neither, for that matter, would have affirmative action. But the last time I checked, we were still living in a world where men control the financing of new businesses, and men are still more comfortable dealing with men. Women who are attracted to the entrepreneurial life—and there are many of us, including those of us who have paid our dues in the male-dominated sectors of American business—still need sharpened skills and ways and means of networking, and this is likely to continue for the foreseeable future.

I mentioned affirmative action for a reason. Racial minorities in our society need their springboards too, and I'm thrilled that there are several initiatives under way, based on our Springboard model, that are attempting to give minority entrepreneurs a leg up. We need them to succeed for the robust health of our society at large. America continues to grow and flourish in good part because of the opportunities it continues to offer newcomers.

In an economic sense, women are "newcomers" too, and the opportunities for us in the fast-changing world economy are enormous.

%,   %,   %,

ONE MAJOR SPUR FOR ME TO WRITE THIS BOOK CAME FROM my publisher, Peter Osnos. When we first met and I told him about Springboard and what we hoped to achieve, he said, "You know, Kay, you've just convinced me that the next Steve Case—the Steve Case of the twenty-first century—is going to be a woman."

Steve Case?

It wasn't our aim when we started Springboard to discover and nurture the next Steve Case. For one thing, there was no predicting Steve Case himself—not twenty-odd years ago when he graduated from Williams College, not ten years ago when, as described in Michael Wolff's *Burn Rate*, "he continued to look like the Procter and Gamble product manager he once was—an affable, nondescript, chinos and button-down guy with a layer of baby fat."

Had Springboard existed in 1985, I'm not at all sure that Case's AmericaOnline would have made our final cut. After all, it took his company seven years to go public (in 1992, with revenues of $30 million and no sign of profitability). And if you'd asked a typical AOL subscriber in the mid-1990s if he thought AOL was the paradigmatic company of the twenty-first century or Steve Case the paradigmatic entrepreneur, that AOL user probably would have laughed uncontrollably—if he didn't punch you in the nose first out of sheer AOL-user frustration.

Yet AOL Time Warner is one of the great communications companies of the twenty-first century, and Steve Case, its "affable, nondescript" chairman, is one of the most powerful men in his field.

I'm hardly the first to notice that there's never been any way of predicting the great corporations or corporate leaders from their entrepreneurial beginnings. (Microsoft's Bill Gates? A computer nerd and college dropout?) And it is way beyond my personal crystal ball to predict if the next Steve Case will be male or female, or black or white or Asian, or have green spiked hair and an earring through his or her eyebrow.

I've written this book simply to show women—*all* women—that we can do it. There are no obstacles on the entrepreneurial journey that can't be overcome. Previous business experience is extremely valuable, but it is not an absolute requirement. Most of the skills involved can be learned, and the smart entrepreneur will recognize her weaknesses and compensate for them by bringing experienced colleagues into her business. Connections are hugely important, but even they can be cultivated. The two factors that seem of paramount importance to me—I would call them prerequisites for any entrepreneur—are (1) the light bulb (the great visionary idea) and (2) the will.

I'd even go so far as to put the second factor first. I don't know where the drive comes from in some of us—that go-for-it-ness, that hunger for the white water—but it's there. I recognized it instantly in Joan Wilbanks, the founder of SecureWorks, the minute she strode onto our stage, first to present her company at the Mid-Atlantic Springboard, then to exhort her "sisters" at the New York and Midwest Boot Camps. It was in her stride, the intensity of her gaze. Different as they are, it glows also in Susan DeFife and in Jill Card and in Jane Homan.

Maybe I recognize it because I know it's in me too. Ever since I was little, I've been one to head right for the obstacles and either go around or over them or, if need be, through them. If you've got that bold spirit in you and you're a woman—and this is what's different today from even a decade or so ago—then there's help out there for you. Lots of it. And there's more coming.

Some dozen years ago, I had a discussion with Reuben Marks, the CEO of Colgate, that I've never forgotten. I was then a rising star in the cable industry and the only female CEO in programming. We were talking about barriers to women rising to the top in corporations and what it was like, as a woman, to take the reins as CEO and sit on the boards of publicly held companies. In the course of our chat, Reuben said something that has ever since rung true to me and has influenced all my actions on behalf of women and minorities.

"Kay, it isn't enough for you to be a role model as CEO," he remarked. "Just because you're the CEO doesn't necessarily get others to realize that women and minorities are worthy of it. You've got to be proactive about what you've done and what you're doing, in order to inspire others to think and act the way you do. If you really believe in helping others, that's your obligation."

As I say, I've never forgotten Reuben's advice. In a very real way, it led to this book.

We're going to keep building our networks—inviting in entrepreneurs, angel investors, venture capitalists, lawyers, financial experts, educational institutions, foundations, and more. We've accelerated the process of bringing women entrepreneurs into the business world of the twenty-first century, and it's working. A very powerful idea—that women can compete in the business arena on an equal footing with men—now has momentum.

%%   %%   %%

I HAVE ONE LAST THOUGHT FOR MY WOMEN READERS. People often ask me how I come up with ideas that change markets. I've done it twice now, in two very different fields—the cable television industry and, more recently, in the raising of capital for women-owned businesses.

The simple truth is that once I get a big, potent idea, it moves me to distraction. I feel compelled to try to move others with me. At the risk of repeating myself, I'm very motivated by the power of ideas, and I've been fortunate enough to persuade others of the power of those ideas too.

Perhaps there's something seductive for me in traveling into the unknown. The journey itself thrills me, and I don't think I'd ever feel altogether happy if I didn't know there was risk involved. Okay, it's risk tempered by hard work and perseverance, but it's surely the risk of the unknown that takes me down class-five white-water rivers and to the top of mountain peaks. And it's not so different, as I've tried to demonstrate, in the business world.

Another way of looking at it is winning. To compete and to win. I think that's all I've ever really wanted to do, and it reminds me of a story Arthur Ashe, the world-class tennis player and first-class humanitarian, once told me about winning.

Arthur had just come from winning Wimbledon in 1985, and he was on his way to play for the Davis Cup on behalf of the United States. Pancho Gonzalez, a former world-class player and coach of the U.S. team, asked Arthur how he was going to win his first match against the Australians.

"Well, I'm number one in the world and I just won Wimbledon," Arthur replied. "I'm going to play my game. You know, serve and volley. Same way I always like to play."

"Wrong!" said Gonzalez, jabbing his finger into Arthur's chest. "You're going to play any damn way you have to play to win!"

That line has always stuck with me: "Play any damn way you have to play to win."

It is perfect advice to the growing class of women who are venturing forth as entrepreneurs, and to all of us who have begun our journeys in the new economic environments of the new century.

Play to win.

May we all be inspired to do just that.

Glossary

Angel Investor who provides capital to a start-up business in its very early stages.

B2B Internet shorthand for "business-to-business"; descriptive term for enterprises that offer their services to other enterprises rather than to consumers.

Balance sheet Formal financial statement that lists and compares the value of a company's assets, liabilities, and owner's **equity.**

Biotech Short for "biotechnology"; refers to the use of biological substances in the manufacture of products that may be used in industries such as genetic engineering, pharmacology, and agriculture.

Book value Value in monetary terms of a company's assets (receivables, cash, inventory, furniture, fixtures, etc.) minus its liabilities (debt), as reflected in its financial statements.

Bootstrapping Self-financing. Term applied to entrepreneurs who start and finance their companies with negligible outside funding.

Burn rate Rate at which a start-up company expends capital to finance costs before attaining profitability. In the heyday of Internet start-ups, sizable burn rates were considered an expression of confidence on the part of a company's investors.

Business model   Schematic plan, or template, by which a company expects to grow and attain profitability. It may or may not be based on the history of other successful enterprises.

Business plan   Formal presentation of an enterprise in a single document.

Cash flow   A company's intake and outflow of cash. When a company's receipts exceed its disbursements, it is said to have a positive cash flow.

Chief executive officer (CEO)   The highest-ranking officer in a company, usually appointed by the board of directors.

Chief financial officer (CFO)   The officer responsible for managing the financial affairs of a company.

Chief operating officer (COO)   Usually the number-two officer, second only to the **CEO,** and responsible for the day-to-day management of a company; usually the president or executive vice president.

Conference pitch   Formal presentation delivered before a sizable audience.

Deal memo   *See* **term sheet.**

Dot-com   Nickname for a commercial on-line company or a company whose Internet address ends in a period followed by "com." On the Internet, "com" stands for "commerce," "org" for "organization," "gov" for "government," and "edu" for "education."

Due diligence   The formal process, often detailed and time-consuming, by which a potential investor investigates a company, assessing and verifying its financial history and prospects.

E-commerce   Business conducted over the Internet. The prefix e- is short for "electronic."

Elevator pitch   Brief presentation that can be delivered in the theoretical minute or less that it takes passengers in an elevator to reach their destination.

Entrepreneur   A person who creates and launches a new business enterprise.

Equity   Ownership interest in a company; also the market value of stock in a company. To have a share in the equity of a business is to own part of it.

Executive summary   Opening section of a business plan, which outlines the enterprise, its history and its goals.

Exit strategy   How investors in a company plan to realize their profits. Sometimes called a "liquidity event," it usually takes the form either of an **initial public offering** (IPO) of stock or a buyout by another company.

High tech   Short for "high technology," it refers to industries or companies that are heavily reliant on new and/or advanced technology for their success.

Income statement   Financial report that lists a company's revenues, expenses, and income over a given period (month, quarter, year) and usually compares those results with previous results and/or forecasts.

Incubator   Organization or individual who gives physical space, technical support, and sometimes financial assistance to fledgling entrepreneurs, usually in exchange for a share in equity.

Initial public offering (IPO)   The process by which shares in a privately held company are offered for sale to the public for the first time.

Letter of intent   *See* **term sheet.**

Leveraged buyout (LBO)   The transaction used to take a public corporation private that is financed through debt such as bank loans and bonds (often high-risk or junk bonds). LBOs are often hostile, made with a minimum of cash and a maximum of incurred debt.

Limited partnership   A shared ownership in which investors have limited liability or responsibility beyond their respective share in the partnership.

Liquidity event   *See* **exit strategy.**

New economy   Sector of the economy involved in new industries, such as software development, the Internet, and biotechnology.

Price-earnings ratio   The ratio of the market price of a share of stock in a company to the company's earnings per share. A high P-E ratio indicates that investors have high expectations for a company's future growth and have bid up the stock's price.

Proprietary assets   The assets owned by a company that are protected either by patent, copyright, or trademark registration.

Return on investment (ROI)   The percentage of profit an investor makes or expects to make on any given investment.

Revenue   Total income generated by a company's business.

Rounds of funding   The various stages at which a start-up company raises money en route to financial stability; typically each successive round, sometimes labeled A, B, C, D, and so on, is meant to generate larger and larger investments.

Scalable   A product or process is said to be scalable when it can be brought quickly and profitably from the prototype or model stage to full-scale production.

Silicon Valley   The geographical area south of San Francisco known for high-tech companies; so-called because of the silicon-chip semiconductor companies that rose to prominence there in the last decades of the twentieth century.

Strategic partnership   Collaboration or joint venture between two or more companies designed to achieve mutually advantageous objectives.

Term sheet   Statement of principal terms in an agreement between two parties, such as a venture capitalist and an entrepreneur. Known in certain fields as a **deal memo** or **letter of intent,** it is a precontract document that, depending on the agreed-to conditions, may or may not have legal standing.

Valuation   The assessment of a company's worth, taking into account both its book value and its potential revenues and profits.

Venture capital   Funds invested in high-risk, high-return enterprises; an investment in a business that is perceived to have excellent growth potential but does not have access to traditional capital markets; type of financing sought by early-stage companies seeking to grow rapidly.

Venture capitalist (VC)   Investor who raises, manages, and invests venture-capital funds, often through the mechanism of **limited partnerships.**

Resources

The following is a list of resources and organizations that offer support to women business owners and entrepreneurs.

National Resources and Organizations

Springboard Enterprises
http://www.springboard2000.org
202-242-6282
debra@springboard2000.org

Entreworld.org
http://www.entreworld.org
816-932-1000
info@entreworld.org

Milken Institute—Emerging Domestic Markets
http://www.milkeninstitute.org
310-998-2600
info@milken-inst.org

Women's Enterprise Institute
http://www.weimidway.org
859-846-5800
info@weimidway.org

National Association of Women's Business Owners
http://www.nawbo.org
301-608-2590

Feminist Majority Foundation
http://www.feminist.org/gateway/1_gatway.html
703-522-2214
femmaj@feminist.org

Center for Women's Business Research
http://www.nfwbo.org
202-638-3060
info@womensbusinessresearch.org

Business and Professional Women/USA
http://www.bpwusa.org
202-293-1100
memberservices@bpwusa.org

Center for International Private Enterprise
http://www.cipe.org
202-721-9200
forum@cipe.org

Institute for Women In Trades, Technology and Science (IWITTS)
http://www.iwitts.com/html/iwitts.html
510-749-0200
donnam@iwitts.com

American Business Women's Association
http://www.abwahq.org

1-800-228-0007
abwa@abwahq.org

Forum for Women Entrepreneurs
http://www.fwe.org
415-970-9000
shannon@fwe.org

National Women Business Owners Corporation
http://www.nwboc.org
800-675-5066
info@wboc.org

The Alliance of Women Entrepreneurs
http://www.awe-westmichigan.org
info@awe-westmichigan.org

Women's Enterprise Development Corporation
http://www.wedc.org
562-983-3747
wedci@wedc.org

ACE-NET
https://ace-net.sr.unh.edu/pub
count-me-in
http://www.count-me-in.org
212-691-6380
info@count-me-in.org

Telecommunication Development Fund's Learning Center
http://www.tdfund.com
202-293-8840
inquiries@tdfund.com

The Committee of 200
http://www.c200.org

312-751-3477
sloeser@c200.org

Women's Business Enterprises National Council
http://www.wbenc.org
202-872-5515
gwhite@wbenc.org

Government Resources

SCORE: Service Corps of Retired Executives
http://www.score.org
1-800-634-0245

Small Business Administration (SBA)
http://www.sba.gov
1-800-U-ASK-SBA
   SBA's Online Women's Business Center
      http://www.onlinewbc.gov
   SBA office of Women's Business Ownership
      http://www.sba.gov/womeninbusiness
   Community Express
      http://www.sba.gov/financing/frcomexp.html
   Microloan Program
      http://www.sba.gov/financing/frmicro.html
   504 Loan Program
      http://www.sba.gov/financing/frcdc504.html

Acknowledgments

Acknowledging all the people who helped make this book happen would truly require a Rolodex because the learning experience that prompted it lasted some thirty years. Hundreds of people contributed to the knowledge I acquired. Many of them may not even realize that their thoughts are woven into the fabric of this book. Others will see their fingerprints quite clearly, and they will know who they are. With a silent tip of the hat to the many who participated along the way, wittingly or not, I will limit myself to those who either played a major role in the events described in the book or who gave me and my collaborator their time and their patience.

I am indebted to Erskine Bowles, who cheered on my quest to open the doors for women entrepreneurs from the very first day. Also, Iris Burnett, a colleague and collaborator who guided me through the halls of Congress and the White House.

Many people participated in forming Springboard. Amy Millman, Cate Muther, Jim Robbins, Denise Brosseau, Karen Bixby, Andrea Silbert, and Trish Costello were there at the creation. Deanna Brown, Pat Cloherty, Mary Hildebrand, Rebecca MacKinnon, Patty Abramson, Amy Wildstein, and Fred Wilson were deeply involved. The book benefited greatly from the generous insights of our intrepid entrepreneurs, whose journeys are chronicled in these pages: Jill Card, Susan DeFife, Jane Homan, and Bruce Brandwen. I gained considerable insight into the world of angel investing from Hans Severeins, John May, and Mario Marino. Personally, Barbara Baldwin, Dana Ortiz, and Olivia Puga were very helpful to me.

Much gratitude is owed to my collaborator, Peter Israel, who has been an absolute delight to work with and who brought wisdom, experience, and an inquisitive mind to this book. My dear friend and literary agent, Joni Evans, was unflagging in her support and encouragement. My publisher, Peter Osnos; editor, Kate Darnton; and copy editor, Ida May B. Norton, all helped bring the idea into first a business deal, then a manuscript, and finally the book you are reading now.

I would like to give tribute to my parents, Bill and Jane Smith, who taught me to be independent from a very early age, kindling the spirit of adventure in my soul. And last, I am indebted to my husband, Billy, who was enormously generous with his time and attention, talking me through the rough spots all along the way.

My thanks to one and all. I couldn't have done it without you.

Index

PUBLICAFFAIRS is a publishing house founded in 1997. It is a tribute to the standards, values, and flair of three persons who have served as mentors to countless reporters, writers, editors, and book people of all kinds, including me.

I. F. STONE, proprietor of *I. F. Stone's Weekly*, combined a commitment to the First Amendment with entrepreneurial zeal and reporting skill and became one of the great independent journalists in American history. At the age of eighty, Izzy published *The Trial of Socrates*, which was a national bestseller. He wrote the book after he taught himself ancient Greek.

BENJAMIN C. BRADLEE was for nearly thirty years the charismatic editorial leader of *The Washington Post*. It was Ben who gave the *Post* the range and courage to pursue such historic issues as Watergate. He supported his reporters with a tenacity that made them fearless, and it is no accident that so many became authors of influential, best-selling books.

ROBERT L. BERNSTEIN, the chief executive of Random House for more than a quarter century, guided one of the nation's premier publishing houses. Bob was personally responsible for many books of political dissent and argument that challenged tyranny around the globe. He is also the founder and was the longtime chair of Human Rights Watch, one of the most respected human rights organizations in the world.

. . .

For fifty years, the banner of Public Affairs Press was carried by its owner, Morris B. Schnapper, who published Gandhi, Nasser, Toynbee, Truman, and about 1,500 other authors. In 1983 Schnapper was described by *The Washington Post* as "a redoubtable gadfly." His legacy will endure in the books to come.

Peter Osnos, *Publisher*